PRAISE FOR *THE CHURCH GUIDE FOR MAKING DECISIONS TOGETHER*

"John Robinson, pastor to the Pilgrims, in his farewell sermon, said, 'for I am verily persuaded the Lord hath more truth and light yet to break forth from His holy word.' This book is for those who are looking for that truth and light. This is not a book for people who want to control the outcome of church meetings but a book for those who want God's truth and light to break forth in our meetings. I heartily commend this work to those who are willing to discover God's presence in community."

—**L. Fitzgerald Reist II**, Former Secretary of the General Conference of The United Methodist Church and Interim Conference Superintendent for Leadership Development in California-Nevada Annual Conference of The United Methodist Church

"Leaders, this book will help you grow community decisions in meetings and give up the process of mostly facilitating arguments. The first time [I used it] I found it daunting, moderating a state meeting of five hundred people, all new to the consensus decision-making process—but once we experienced it I knew we could not go back to the old way of doing things. Since then I have used the process in all kinds of settings where decisions are made. How grateful I was that the Uniting Church uses this decision-making process, for a decade later I found myself presiding over the Triennial National Assembly addressing the issue of ordination and homosexuality in a community and pastoral way."

—**Dean Drayton**, Past President of the Uniting Church in Australia (2003–2006)

"For about a decade, my denomination has used at many of its meetings beyond the congregational level a version of the consensus-based approach these authors advocate. The result—a more inclusive decision-making process and a greater ownership of the decisions made."

—**John H. Young**, Executive Minster, Theological Leadership / Ministre exécutif, direction théologique, The United Church of Canada / L'Église Unie du Canada

"The authors not only bring skilled observations to the challenges of church decision-making, they also offer hope and practical tools for moving beyond *Robert's Rules of Order* and escalated conflict to community discernment that births consensus and hope for church decision-making. A valuable tool for all pastors, church leadership, and members."

—**Edward Hammett**, Professional Certified Coach, Church and Leadership Coach for Cooperative Baptist Fellowship of North Carolina, author of *Reaching People under 30 While Keeping People over 60*, and president of Transforming Solutions

TERENCE CORKIN AND
JULIA KUHN WALLACE

THE CHURCH GUIDE FOR MAKING DECISIONS TOGETHER

Abingdon Press™

Nashville

THE CHURCH GUIDE FOR MAKING DECISIONS TOGETHER

Copyright © 2017 by Abingdon Press

Library of Congress Cataloging-in-Publication Data has been requested.

ISBN: 978-1-5018-3807-1

17 18 19 20 21 22 23 24 25 26—10 9 8 7 6 5 4 3 2 1

MANUFACTURED IN THE UNITED STATES OF AMERICA

Julia
For Steve and my children—Josh and Amanda—and my grandchildren—Collin,
Christian, and Ava Grace—as well as the congregations that I have worked with over
the years. You have given me the courage to live out the practices described in this book.
May you grow faithfully as disciples of Jesus Christ in a community ever-committed to
discerning and doing the will of God.

Terence
For my family: Julie and our children—Rebecca, Natalie, and Monique—and our
lovely grandchildren—William, Sienna, and Lauren; and my brothers and sisters
in Christ, that they may learn the gifts and graces that God has given us to be
in community as faithful disciples of Jesus Christ.

CONTENTS

CONTENTS

ACKNOWLEDGMENTS

In our experience, Christians care what God thinks and wants for and from us. Somehow in the minutiae of ministry we find ourselves in inadequate processes to make decisions. So, we resort to popular votes, following the loudest voice and wondering if there is a more spiritual way. There is!

We wrote this book for the many colleagues who have shared stories of church fights over something as simple as the color of church tiles or as major as whether to keep their pastor. This book is for the people who never lost the belief that we can do better than this; and as they wrestled with the limitations of *Robert's Rules of Order* they continued to hope that they could operate in a more respectful, engaging, and open way with one another.

We thank them for their courage and hopefulness and for sharing their heartfelt stories with us.

Our hopes and uses for this book include the following:

- to provide an effective process to use at the local and judicatory church levels
- to be a definitive resource in seminary and college classes training pastors
- to assist facilitators as they lead faith communities to discern God's will together

This book is dedicated to all of those who yearn to work together to discern God's will in the midst of making decisions.

You may contact us at julia@makingchurchdecisions.com and terence @makingchurchdecisions.com with any questions or comments. We look forward to hearing from you.

SO WHAT'S WRONG WITH THE WAY WE MAKE DECISIONS?

It was the worst church meeting that I have ever been to in my life (and I have been to a lot of challenging meetings)! At an international ecumenical gathering, an experienced General Secretary of a National Council of Churches stood at the microphone and shouted abuse at the chairperson of a committee who had just presented a major report. The speaker was expressing his opposition to the recommendation in the report yet seemed out of control. The meeting chair sought to call him to order, yet the man refused to comply. For over five minutes there was vitriol and defiance of proper process. Then others joined in on both sides of the debate with equal vehemence. Things quickly spiraled out of control.

While no one would suggest that this man was following the established rules of the meeting when he ignored the chair's ruling, the question lingers: What was it that made this person think that this kind of behavior was acceptable in a church forum? What kind of values and practices guide decision-making in his home church that says it is OK to shout, denigrate, and question the integrity of people who have a different point of view? Something is seriously wrong when senior leaders in the church think that all that matters in a meeting is getting their way in any way that they can!

Many mainline churches are experiencing growing incivility, including non-physical forms of violence, as their members engage with one another around matters over which they have very strong feelings. In many places, people have become acclimatized to this kind of behavior, to the point where it goes unchallenged. The behavior is accepted even though there are many participants in these meetings who are dismayed and hurt by these "winner takes all" tactics.

Yet notwithstanding that many a church meeting has the character of the "shootout at the OK Corral," many people expect better. They expect churches to use more spiritual ways of deciding matters, and they are disappointed to find political maneuvering and aggressive, demeaning practices running rampant in meetings. Is it any wonder that meeting attendance is down and it is increasingly difficult to find leaders who will volunteer for service in such circumstances?

The politicized atmosphere of many church meetings has led to a breakdown of trust and to people disengaging from the life and mission of the church. The prevailing meeting rules that are used in many churches and community groups are inherently polarizing and politicized. The adversarial style that is causing so much hurt and harm in the life of churches is known as parliamentary procedure or *Robert's Rules of Order*. The process cares little, if at all, for the values that the church community says that it stands for.

Many individuals do not fully know how to engage *Robert's Rules of Order*, which restricts the number of people who can participate. The parliamentary process gives primacy to a majority getting their way on a particular issue—even if that majority is only 50 percent + 1. Such a majority is not a decision; it's a division! As we all know very well, when a contentious issue is resolved with a significant minority feeling alienated by the result, the number of people who own or are willing to live and work with the final decision is greatly reduced. Frequently this means that the issue arises again and again for reconsideration. Repeating such debates sustains conflict in a group, is debilitating, and distracts people from the true mission of the church.

Not only does the parliamentary process have the objective of creating winners and losers; it also disrespects and devalues alternative ways of developing insight and making decisions. These alternative ways of understanding are socially, culturally, and relationally more appropriate in today's society.

Culturally and linguistically diverse church communities make decisions through processes that are very different to a parliamentary process. Long and careful conversations take place before an action is decided upon. Issues are explored through patterns of conversation that are very different to the direct and confrontational style of parliamentary debating. The increased participation of women in the meetings of the church has led to a significant number of people wanting a more collaborative rather than combative way of making decisions. Millennials don't relate to *Robert's Rules of Order* as a way of developing insight, sharing opinions, and finding solutions.

Society has moved, even in traditionally democratic societies, to increasingly participatory processes in many areas of life; and as such, people are not happy to be told what to do. The expectation for inclusion in the decisions that affect them frequently leads to people not accepting or fully owning decisions made for them by others. The character and practice of social media make it abundantly clear that people want to be actively engaged in the things that matter to them. Bystanders are few and far between; participants are everywhere.

In a parliamentary process of decision-making, primacy is given to reason and logical argument. Reason and logic, in that world, validate a conclusion and are the arbiters of what constitutes wisdom. How many times have we heard it said with disdain in church meetings, "Oh, he is so emotional. I wish he would just get to the point!"? It is as though emotion, story, and experience have nothing to offer in the search for insight, wisdom, and meaning. How far this is from the truth!

The social tide is turning, and many people familiar with the traditional way of doing business are getting nervous that change is in the air. The hegemony of western rationalist wisdom has collapsed. Despite the rear-guard action of the proponents of parliamentary decision-making styles, the fact is that it no longer holds the ground uncontested. Experience, feelings, and storytelling have moved to the center of where people find insight, wisdom, and meaning. However, like King Canute who thought that he could hold back the tide by the power of his commanding words, supporters of the parliamentary procedure in church decision-making seek to prevent the inevitable tide of change by ever-stronger commands to "stop."

THANKFULLY, THERE IS AN ALTERNATIVE!

A consensus-building approach is a better social and cultural fit these days for a church board or committee or congregation or church judicatory body to discern the will of God for its life. A true consensus-building approach

- creates an environment in which people are able to name what is important for them in the issue that is before the meeting

- assists everyone in gaining a full understanding of the issues and the consequences of any decision that is taken

- collaboratively generates options and helps participants come to a place where they can accept the views of the majority even if they are not their first choice

- allows people to know that they have been respected and taken seriously

Many church members and leaders want a new way of making decisions—a way that honors diversity, respects all participants, is collaborative, builds a sense of community, and uses time wisely. What is lacking is a step-by-step guide that assists them to

- articulate their experience of what is, and a vision for what might be

- understand how to prepare for an alternative way of decision-making

- develop and use the procedures and tools that meeting presiders need in order to create a consensus-building model of decision-making

This is why we wrote this book.

There are many books that have been written on discernment. Throughout the history and breadth of the Christian tradition saints, sages, mystics, and theologians have offered their insights into the ways of experiencing the leading of God. The approach taken in this book does not seek to negate these disciplines. The spiritual disciplines that are affirmed in the literature on discernment are essential grounding and necessary practices so that people are prepared to participate in a discernment process. This process is different because it addresses itself to group disciplines and practices that work toward *corporate* rather than *individual* discernment.

This book starts from the premise that when a Christian community gathers to make decisions, it has one goal: *to understand the will of God in this specific matter for this community, at this time and in this place.* There have been many ways in which such discernment has been sought. Traditional processes such as *Robert's Rules of Order* may be understood as a way in which a community decides what God wants it to do. At issue is what process best serves the community today in its quest to make good decisions, and to do so in ways that are consistent with its Christian character. This book makes the case that a consensus-building approach best positions the church to discern the will of God and allows it to operate in a way that is consistent with its Christian character. We are offering an approach that can be used in any church context—from the local board to larger denominational gatherings—and can function within the structures of any church polity.

No one process can claim to be discernment. However, it is a fact that some processes are more likely to lead to a faithful discerning of God's will. Approaches that are faithful to this goal will be effective because they draw on a wide range of Christian practices and processes that are coherent with both the contemporary culture and the values of the Christian community. The process outlined in this book is the journey or strategy to reach the place called discernment. This consensus-building process respects local contexts and draws on culturally relevant practices that are based solidly in Christian values. In the Christian community, discernment is the place where that community can say that they believe they have discerned God's will *for this community, at this time and in this place.*

As you reflect on your current approach for making decisions, decide what is unhelpful and what can be done better. Do you use *Robert's Rules of Order?*

The limitations of *Robert's Rules of Order* include the following:

- Well-educated males who operate in an intellectually linear manner and who are articulate in presenting their views are privileged.

- Vocal people who think fast on their feet and who are not shy at offering their opinions gain an advantage.

- As a parliamentary model, it fails to recognize and value other ways of knowing or alternative ways of exploring issues, which renders mute many voices.

- A status quo approach, it devalues alternative modes of decision-making used in other cultures, which increased gender sensitivity teaches many people to appreciate.

- By focusing on a piece of legislation, the parliamentary model does not assist exploration of the issues behind the words thus narrowing the discussion. So the possible outcomes are limited from the start.

- Parliamentary procedures assume a "for" or "against" position, which is an artificial polarity that does not align with the way most decisions are reached in real life.

- The dominant parliamentary model operates in a way that is inherently oppositional and combative and therefore not collaborative.

- The operational framework of parliamentary procedures is about winning the argument at all costs.

- *Robert's Rules of Order* disempower a significant percentage of people who don't understand the complex rules and get lost in procedure. This creates confusion and alienation.

- *Robert's Rules of Order* are particularly problematic in complex matters because they force people to take sides even before they feel they have understood the complexity of the issue.

In contrast, a consensus-building approach:

- creates an environment in which people are able to name what is important for them in the issue

- provides the time necessary to gain a full understanding of the issues and the consequences that result from a decision

- generates options and facilitates collaboration in developing a response to issues

- respects and values a variety of ways in which insight is reached, for example, through the telling of stories, the acknowledgment of feelings, and the owning of hopes and fears

- encourages acceptance of the views of the majority even if they are not an individual's first choice

- ensures that people have been understood, respected, and taken seriously

We believe that many people want a new way of making decisions—a way that honors diversity, respects all participants, is collaborative, and builds community.

This resource helps leaders articulate their experience of the limitations in the present system and provides a vision for an alternative approach. This book offers you a way to create an alternative way of decision-making that is based on Christian values. It includes details of meeting procedures and tools that can be used to build consensus.

Church traditions have different processes and cultures, so it is important that any consensus-building process is adaptable to these various contexts. The model proposed can be accommodated to any church's way of making decisions. This book provides the tools that allow church organizations to craft a consensus-based approach that is values driven, while meeting their particular cultural practices and legal requirements.

WHAT IS CONSENSUS?

Consensus has many different connotations for people. It is also a word that can be used in two very different ways. More will be said throughout this book on many aspects of consensus, but at this point it is appropriate to say something about how the term is being used in this context.

Frequently consensus is used to denote that the members of a group have reached a unanimous view. In this situation people say things such as, "The group made the decision by consensus" or "There was consensus that A, B, and C should happen." Consensus used in this a way describes a way of making a decision.

There are many ways that a group might make a decision: by majority, by random choice, by agreeing to accept the advice of experts, by consensus, and so on. The following YouTube clip illustrates different kinds of decision-making. In this clip, consensus is understood to mean unanimity: https:// www.youtube.com/watch?v=cbvLOOo3NHc.

However, consensus is not just a way of making a decision. It is also a way of engaging in the exploration of an issue—a methodology that assumes certain commitments and practices. Apparently the characters on the television series *Gilmore Girls* do consensus in this sense, as you can see from the following clip: https://www.youtube.com/watch?v=Xwf99ZhAViU. We are not recommending their rushed style or all that they do. However, it is a nice illustration of consensus when it is understood as a way for a group to go about developing its position. This is a process that listens to all points of view on what the participants think is important, shares many perspectives, includes consideration of all the relevant facts and feelings, and weighs them all before a decision is made. Interestingly, in this clip one person makes the decision even though the process for looking at the issues was a consensus style.

Throughout this book the focus is on the process a group uses before it comes to the point of making a decision. The language used most often is "a consensus-building approach." We understand very well that in some contexts it is not possible to change the rules of the group so that a decision can only be taken by consensus. So consensus as a way of making the decision is not assumed. Nevertheless, it is always possible to use processes that move a group toward consensus even if the rule by which a decision must be taken is by a vote or by one person in authority. This book advocates that the most theologically sound, sociologically relevant, culturally appropriate, and faith-encouraging way for churches to make decisions is to use processes and tools that build consensus, irrespective of the way the final decision is made.

Consensus in this context does not mean unanimity. Consensus means the way of being in community while seeking to discern the will of God. It is a way of being in community that builds a response to an issue through the involvement of all. It is collaborative, comprehensive in addressing the issues, and opens up new insights.

Reaching true discernment is like arriving at a destination by drawing on a wide range of practices from the Christian tradition, practices that are coherent with the values of the Christian community as well as culturally appropriate. Here is a map for the journey that will enable a faith community to reach the place called discernment.

Come on this journey with us. You will be so pleased that you did!

CHAPTER 1

THE GOAL AND CHARACTER OF CHRISTIAN DECISION-MAKING

There is a scene in Lewis Carroll's classic book *Alice in Wonderland* in which Alice is lost, not an unusual thing for Alice. When she reaches a fork in the road there is a large tree and sitting in the tree is a smiling Cheshire cat. Alice starts talking to the cat and finally asks which fork in the road she should take. The cat answers, "Well, that very much depends on where you want to go." To which Alice replies, "I don't really care where I go." The cat then says, "Then it doesn't very much matter which road you take."

The destination shapes the journey. Without a clear end in sight then every journey becomes a random collection of steps and turns. With a clear purpose there is meaning to our activities, and the things that we do make sense. So it is with church meetings. When people meet with a clear understanding about the goal of Christian decision-making, and the character that should be demonstrated as they go about it, then they know what steps they need to take. If churches don't care about what they are doing and how they do it, then any way of doing business—any path—is as good as another.

Many congregations have lost sight of their purpose and so have settled for ways of doing business that are at odds with the purpose of Christian decision-making. Sadly, the way many church members behave is also at variance with what should be expected of Christians when they meet. If people are concerned about the goal and character of Christian decision-making,

1

they will take one path. If they do not care about these things, then they can take any path they like.

What do you think is the purpose of church meetings?

What behavior is appropriate for people in church meetings?

When I first began my ordained ministry, I was in a parish served by two ministers. We took turns leading the bimonthly meeting of the parish council. When I was chairing the meeting we always finished the meeting early. At that time, I thought a fast meeting was a good meeting! Let's just get the business done! My colleague, however, was very different. Bill loved to let people talk things through, often in a roundabout way. He let them talk about why they thought this or thought that. One night as I sat at the back of the room the clock raced toward 10:00 p.m., with much of the agenda still before us. My colleague let a person ramble on and on without, it seemed to me, ever getting to the point. When the speech ended I thought to myself, "If Bill lets anyone tell one more story I am going to scream!" He did.

I thought the real purpose of a meeting (church or otherwise) was simple. Follow an agenda and finish quickly. Meeting agendas were like grocery shopping lists: just tick off items as completed, and get out of there as fast as you can. My understanding of the purpose of a meeting was to help the church make good decisions and to run efficiently. My leadership style in the meetings reflected that view. We would get to the "facts"; keep focused on the issue before us; and as soon as it was clear where the majority was ready to go, we would vote and move on. That kind of efficient meeting was the only one that I had ever experienced. For me it was the benchmark of a good meeting.

Every meeting of the parish council began with prayer and reflections on scripture. The room was full of faithful servants of Christ giving their best for the service of God and the church. On occasions, we were self-consciously aware of the gifts of scripture and prayer as we navigated some of the more difficult decisions. Sadly, though, I do not think that we were profoundly aware of the theological understanding of what we were doing on all those long Wednesday evenings, nor the impact they would have on the community.

If we had seriously thought about it, and tried to put into theological terms; what we were trying to accomplish was to understand what Jesus wanted from his people gathered in that place. This was not simply a meeting that we were engaged in; it was part of God's unfolding drama of salvation. Our parish council meeting was caught up in the divine purposes of God. If only we would listen carefully then we would hear Christ guiding us in the ways of faithfulness. Awesome!

The Christian community makes an audacious claim. The church asserts that it is possible to know the will of God. Every Sunday in pulpits, grass clearings, in homes and meeting halls, preachers testify the world over to what God has done in Jesus Christ and the implications of that activity for the people gathered. Unless the church can lay claim to the possibility of knowing the will of God, then it has nothing significant or relevant to say to believers and nonbelievers alike.

When Christians meet to make decisions, they are living out of the same profound confidence: God will lead us. Our church meetings have a destination. The endpoint of a church meeting is to understand the will of God for this community, at this time and in this place. The ultimate goal is more than just taking care of business. With the destination (discernment) in mind, it is abundantly clear that the path that one takes makes a huge difference to whether that goal will be reached. The meeting practices of the church serve or hinder the objective of discerning the will of God. Without the objective of seeking to be obedient to Jesus Christ, the sovereign head of the church, our meetings are meaningless. Without seeking to be attentive and responsive to the leading of the Holy Spirit, our meetings are a waste of time.

The first premise of the Christian life is that God can be known and that God's will for us can be revealed. God's work in Jesus makes it possible to have unity with God and to be obedient. All the barriers that prevent this relationship and capacity to faithfully follow God's way have been overcome. Through the work of the Holy Spirit, people are sustained in relationship with Christ, invited to serve God and empowered to do so.

If the first premise is that God can be known and followed, then the corollary is that there are means through which it is possible for God to mediate God's will to humanity. Theologians, starting with the Apostle Paul, along with mystics, bishops, scholars, numerous theological schools, and human experience, have addressed themselves to the question of how God is revealed to us. The purpose of this book is more modestly focused on how the will of God might be revealed through a particular community's decision-making processes. The point of commonality between mystics, theologians, the scriptures, and meeting planners is that there is a necessary and shared objective for all Christians and that is to seek to understand—to discern—the will of God. It is vital that we keep this goal as the priority!

3

Discernment (making Godly decisions together) is the goal, the purpose, and the conclusion. Discernment is the place that makes sense of all the steps along the way. Absent the goal of discernment, then church meetings are rambles through terrain that is neither interesting nor relevant. However, when true discernment (knowing the will of Christ for his church) is constantly before church meetings, then it is possible to evaluate everything that we do against the test of its usefulness in reaching discernment. A ready reference point for anyone in a meeting of the church is whether the conversations, the meeting processes used, the agenda, and so on, are contributing to helping people know what Jesus wants of us. If the processes do this, then by all means continue with them. But if they do not, then surely they need to be put aside. By intentionally putting ourselves in the best place where we can be caught up into the saving purposes of God for all of creation, our meetings are transformed. We view the process we use to make decisions differently—as holy—and we choose what behaviors are appropriate in that setting.

Most church leaders have their rules that guide their meeting procedures. This book offers an alternative guide or template to ensure that meetings are productive and that the decisions made are far more inclusive, participatory, owned by the group, and so far more likely to actually be implemented.

If knowing the will of God were that easy, then everyone would be doing it. It isn't easy for theological, sociological, capacity, and willingness reasons. However whether it is easy or not, there is no other game in town for the Christian. If we are not interested in discerning the will of God for our community, at this time and in this place, then why should we hold any church meetings? There are many answers to this question, but people are usually reluctant to voice them out loud. Sometimes people run church meetings to support their personal or family interests. At other times people hold meetings to marshal the resources of the congregation in support of their personal pet project regardless of what the majority of members may want. People's motivations are also varied: they seek control, power, and influence. In short, people like to get their way! When these are the goals of church meetings, different rules apply.

When congregations or judicatories meet together to seek discernment, the theological affirmation of most Protestant Christians is that we are more likely to discern the will of God in community than if we try and work it out on our own. The practices of Christian discernment are best accomplished in community. Yet it seems that many Christians like to make their decisions in private based on their own reading of scripture or what seems good to them. However, faithful discipleship will occur when the group takes into account the views of all those who are in the meeting, attends to the scriptures, brings its best thinking to the discussion, and listens to the tradition of the church as reflected in ecumenical and historical perspectives. Do you see the difference?

Discernment doesn't just happen! There are things that can be done that help or hinder discernment. Much more will be said on this subject throughout this book. However, at this junction, it is worth making the point that discernment requires that sound judgment be exercised, sensitivity exhibited, and wisdom applied. Also, discernment is profoundly contextual.

Among major world religions, Christianity is unique in its claim that God—in all God's fullness—was present in a human being in a particular place and time. God was in Christ reconciling the world to God's self (2 Corinthians 5:18, 19). This is the doctrine of the incarnation, and it has profound implications for understanding how Christians seek to reach an awareness of the will of God.

Jesus of Nazareth was born of Mary, walked the hills of Galilee and the cities of the Decapolis, and suffered under Pontius Pilate. He was located in a specific time and place. Jesus' faithfulness was expressed in the context of the world. Faithfulness to God only makes sense in the Christian tradition if it is expressed in the here and now. Therefore, to speak of discernment in the Christian tradition is not to speak of some rarefied insight into a cosmic consciousness or insight into the end of time. Christian discernment is about understanding and accepting what God wants from us. The value and necessity of discernment is precisely because it is incarnational; it is about doing the right thing by God. Like Jesus, the church—the body of Christ—must find the way of knowing the will of God and doing it. Faithfulness depends on it!

Certainly, any good discernment process needs to accept the limitations of human frailty and sinfulness. Christians can and do aim to get to a point where there is a common and widely held view on what God thinks about a specific issue or matter. Yet as soon as one says that out loud, it becomes hard to list too many topics on which there is universal agreement among Christians even though all are faithfully seeking the will of God. However, where there is disagreement on these important topics, it is not because one group of people is faithful and the other side is just stubborn and unwilling to follow the Lord. When Christians are divided, it happens even after people of faith and goodwill have earnestly read the scriptures, prayed, and discussed the matter together. Disagreements are the human experience of the church down through the ages. They arise even when everyone involved is trying their best to seek the will of Christ for his church. This reality should encourage every Christian to a high degree of humility and a willingness to be quite modest in their claims for having every issue all sorted out. The proof of this humility is in the way we treat one another with utmost respect even in the midst of differences. This is why the manner in which we listen and seek to understand one another is important.

The goal of Christian decision-making is to put people of faith in a place where they can participate in the hopes and purposes that God has in store for the community of which they are a part. That community may be very specific and focused on a task influenced by where they live; it may be a local congregation or even the wider denomination; it may be a concern for the town or country in which they live; or it could be about broader principles that should be affirmed. Whatever the particular situation in which you find yourself, God is looking for a partner and wants to include you in the reconciling work of Christ's ministry. Effective Christian meeting practices put people of faith in the best place where they can discern the will of God for their community.

THE CHARACTER OF CHRISTIAN DECISION-MAKING

One of the major obstacles to the evangelical task of the church is the long and sordid parade of times when the church operated on the assumption that the ends justified the means. In the name of noble and worthy causes, the church has behaved in barbarous and evil ways that judged people and alienated others. The memories of when the grand and high-sounding objectives of the church led to war, murder, treachery, violence, and all manner of evils continues to hamstring the evangelical task of the church in many places today. The end never justifies the means! The necessary conclusion is to say that the process through which the church makes decisions matters as much as the decision that is made. Anyone who suggests that the church can use any method to reach a decision so long as it is the "right" one, has failed to learn the lessons of history.

Many individuals and communities still refuse to open their ears to the gospel because of the way they have been treated by the church and individual believers in the past. Who can blame them? There are many Christians who have left their local congregation, and sometimes their faith, because Christians have behaved in ways that are not consistent with what the church says it stands for. Therefore, faithfully running church meetings is a priority for anyone who is interested in the evangelical task of the church. Yet many evangelicals want to play off the decision against the process that leads to it. Getting the right decision by a process that alienates, hurts, disrespects, and offends other Christians is not in the best interests of the mission of the church. A faithful decision reached faithfully is the best approach. To any who may be asking the question whether process matters, the answer is yes, it most certainly does!

The means used by the church to reach its decisions must be coherent with the ends that the church serves. Character matters. The church must behave in a way that is consistent with what it says about God, itself, and the Christian community. If its behavior is not consistent with its values, then it does not matter whether it has discerned the will of God or not, because the witness of the church will be materially diminished.

Seeking to discern the will of God is a noble enterprise. It is a goal worthy of striving for together. This goal does not justify that any means may be used to reach it. If the process used to discern the will of God does not enhance the prospect of discernment and look like the church at work, then the witness of the church is diminished. Look at the news headlines after some national church meetings. Do they always provide a credible Christian witness, or do they alienate and divide people?

There are many scripture readings that speak about the character of God and the manner in which the members of the Christian community are meant to interact with one another. Here are two examples from the Apostle Paul:

> Therefore, as a prisoner for the Lord, I encourage you to live as people worthy of the call you received from God. Conduct yourselves with all humility, gentleness, and patience. Accept each other with love, and make an effort to preserve the unity of the Spirit with the peace that ties you together. You are one body and one spirit, just as God also called you in one hope. There is one Lord, one faith, one baptism, and one God and Father of all, who is over all, through all, and in all. (Ephesians 4:1-6)

7

Love is patient, love is kind, it isn't jealous, it doesn't brag, it isn't arrogant, it isn't rude, it doesn't seek its own advantage, it isn't irritable, it doesn't keep a record of complaints, it isn't happy with injustice, but it is happy with the truth. (1 Corinthians 13:4-6)

Thinking about some of the church meetings observed over the years we think it is a wonderful thing when those gathered recognize one another as one body and are humble, gentle, and patient as they bear with one another in love. It's a beautiful thing when there is no envy, boasting, or pride; when there is an honoring of others without them being easily angered or self-seeking; and when truth-seeking takes place alongside protecting one another, trusting, hoping, and persevering.

It is no secret what the character of the Christian community is meant to be. What seems harder for Christians to understand is how to order the life of the church so that these characteristics are encouraged and developed, and their opposites discouraged or discontinued. There seems to be no harder place to live the character of the Christian life than in the business meetings of the church. Too often people attending our meetings do not say, "Look at these Christians. See how much they love one another!"

Of course when Christians are passionate about important things there will be energy in the room. People bring all their energy, fears, hopes, preconceived ideas, and anxieties to a meeting. This is natural and can make a positive contribution toward discernment. Yet when the satisfaction of these passions, the release of this energy, the assuaging of these fears, the realizing of hopes, getting one's way, and the release of anxieties become the purpose of the meeting, rather than discernment, then the character of the Christian community easily goes out the window.

People come to meetings with all kinds of games in mind—that the truth will be declared, that they will get their way, that some will win and others will lose, that personal gain will be realized, and so on. When these ends become all that matters, then it is impossible that discernment is done in a way that is consistent with the things we say about God, the Christian community, and ourselves.

An alternative starting point is the theological affirmation that the people present in the room are called and gifted by God for the purpose of leadership. This perspective starts with an expectation that people will behave in a way that is consistent with Christian values and behaviors. This way is then shaped by meeting processes, which support the expression of these values and the practices of the Christian faith, and which enable them to be realized.

DISCERNMENT IN CONTEXT

The Christian faith is inherently incarnational. God's Christ is known as Jesus of Nazareth because he lived in a certain town; fed on a local diet; and was shaped by, and responded to, a specific sociopolitical, economic, and religious environment. The doctrine of the incarnation puts context to the forefront of what faithfulness looks like. There is no faithfulness that does not express itself in a specific time and place with all the baggage that goes with that.

Structures and systems have been changing over the centuries, and some patterns have become limiting or nonfunctional as the context in which they were operating changed. In their place new social structures and systems have been able to flourish. Some of these patterns of social behavior are adaptations of earlier models, and some are very different.

In short, the people and religious organizations that will survive into the future will do so by reframing what it means to be a Christian community of disciples, remembering the importance of discerning God's will, and finding effective ways to make decisions while reclaiming a passionate mission.

Unless attention is paid to the social context in which the Christian community is operating, it runs the risk of continuing to operate in a way that has passed its "use-by date." If the decision-making processes that are in use today were built for a setting that no longer exists, then these processes are on their way to extinction. The consensus-building process commended in this book is a process whose time has come and can truly prosper in the present environment.

Failure by the church to look closely at the social context in which its business procedures were developed, and testing their ongoing relevance for these times, leaves the church open to becoming ineffective at discernment.

Many examples exist of how a changing context led to adaptive change in the way that authority was exercised and how decisions were made. Examples include the period where there was no questioning of the absolute right of kings; in the later European feudal period, the senior barons began to exercise influence in the decision-making process; in many traditional

Australian, Pacific, and African cultures, the men talk at length until the elders decide what the community will do; then there is the parliamentary model.

Not one of these models of decision-making should be idealized, and neither should they be demonized. They worked in their historical and cultural context. However, the context changed, and the social setting, the dominant values in the community, and the goals of decision-making changed to the extent that they no longer worked as well as they used to do. Indeed some have become totally untenable as ways of making decisions in a lot of places today. At the time when the disjunction between the old environment and the new was at its greatest tension, and a new way of making decisions had not been negotiated, there has been a lot of pain and disagreement. It is the stuff of which revolutions are made.

The parliamentary approach in its time was a significant step and had much to commend it to the emerging cultures of European and Northern American society. Accordingly, *Robert's Rules of Order* found acceptance in the churches even though its processes ignored Christian approaches to discernment and the character of Christian community. There has been a massive change in the environment between when *Robert's Rules of Order* commenced and the social and cultural environment that operates today. Even though changes in the way of decision-making are potentially disorienting and can cause a lot of tension, the church must discover new and effective ways to make decisions. That approach is available—the time for a consensus-building approach has come.

THE PEOPLE OF GOD HAVE USED MANY DIFFERENT METHODS OF DISCERNMENT

Throughout the scriptures it is evident that the will of God has been discerned in a wide variety of ways. Each has been accepted because it made sense within the cultural and social environment of its time. Are you willing to accept that they were a means of discerning the will of God in their time, but wondering whether all of them would be acceptable methodologies in a local congregational meeting today?

1. DIRECT MEDIATION OF INFORMATION BY A GOD-APPOINTED LEADER

Moses went up to God. The LORD called to him from the mountain, "This is what you should say to Jacob's household and declare to the Israelites: So Moses came down, called together the people's elders, and set before them all these words that the LORD had commanded him. The people all responded with one voice: "Everything that the Lord has said we will do." Moses reported to the Lord what the people said. (Exodus 19:3, 7, 8)

The prophets: "Thus says the Lord . . .

And in the Gospels:

As Jesus passed alongside the Galilee Sea, he saw two brothers, Simon and Andrew, throwing fishing nets into the sea, for they were fishermen. "Come, follow me," he said, "and I'll show you how to fish for people." Right away, they left their nets and followed him. After going a little farther, he saw James and John, Zebedee's sons, in their boat repairing the fishing nets. At that very moment he called them. They followed him, leaving their father Zebedee in the boat with the hired workers. (Mark 1:16-20)

2. RELIGIOUS RITES

Then Saul asked the LORD God of Israel, "Why haven't you answered your servant today? If the wrongdoing is mine or my son Jonathan's, respond with Urim, but if the wrongdoing belongs to your people Israel, respond with Thummim." Jonathan and Saul were taken by lot, and the troops were cleared. (1 Samuel 14:41)

After he took his seat at the table with them, he took the bread, blessed and broke it, and gave it to them. Their eyes were opened and they recognized him, but he disappeared from their sight. They said to each other, "Weren't our hearts on fire when he spoke to us along the road and when he explained the scriptures for us?" They got up right then and returned to Jerusalem. They found the eleven and their companions gathered together. They were saying to each other, "The Lord really has risen! He appeared to Simon!" Then the two disciples described what had happened along the road and how Jesus was made known to them as he broke the bread. (Luke 24:30–35)

11

3. MYSTIC EXPERIENCES

In the year of King Uzziah's death, I saw the Lord sitting on a high and exalted throne, the edges of his robe filling the temple. Winged creatures were stationed around him. Each had six wings: with two they veiled their faces, with two their feet, and with two they flew about. Then I heard the Lord's voice saying, "Whom should I send, and who will go for us?" I said, "I'm here; send me." (Isaiah 6:1-2, 8)

A revelation of Jesus Christ, which God gave him to show his servants what must soon take place. Christ made it known by sending it through his angel to his servant John, who bore witness to the word of God and to the witness of Jesus Christ, including all that John saw. (Revelation 1:1-2)

4. HOLDING A CONFERENCE

Paul and Barnabas took sides against these Judeans and argued strongly against their position. The church at Antioch appointed Paul, Barnabas, and several others from Antioch to go up to Jerusalem to set this question before the apostles and the elders. The apostles and the elders gathered to consider this matter. After much debate, Peter stood and addressed them, "Fellow believers, you know that, early on, God chose me from among you as the one through whom the Gentiles would hear the word of the gospel and come to believe. The entire assembly fell quiet as they listened to Barnabas and Paul describe all the signs and wonders God did among the Gentiles through their activity. (Acts 15:2, 6, 7, 12)

The way to decide which methodology is best suited to your situation is to ask the following questions:

- What is the goal of Christian decision-making?
- Do the methods that you use to make decisions reflect what you believe about the character of God and Christian behavior?
- Are the meeting methods that you currently use theologically, culturally, and sociologically appropriate for the time and place in which you live?

In this chapter we have encouraged you to see that the traditional parliamentary style of decision-making is doing more harm than good. We are challenging you to think about the purpose of church meetings and how they can be shaped to reflect Christian character.

There is a process that addresses all these questions in a faithful and effective way. In subsequent chapters we explore how to understand, design, and implement a consensus-building decision-making process in your church.

REFLECTION QUESTIONS

1. Answer the questions on page 12. Do your responses indicate that you are using an appropriate process to make decisions? What changes could you make to better align your process with the character of the church?

2. (a) Review the scripture passages listed in this chapter. What do they say to you about God? About God's people?
(b) What other Bible passage(s) would you add to this list?

3. Think back to the last important meeting you attended. How would you describe the process used? Were people able to participate? Was the meeting chaotic or well structured? Was a decision made? Will it be implemented?

4. Think of leaders that you admire. How do they run meetings? What do you learn from their example? What does their behavior suggest about the character of the church?

FROM CONFLICT TO CONSENSUS

Supporting Transformative Decision-Making

Courage is what it takes to stand up and speak.
Courage is also what it takes to sit down and listen.

—Winston Churchill

Any fool can know. The point is to understand.

—Albert Einstein

Conflict is inevitable, but combat is optional.

—Max Lucado

WHEN CONFLICT HAPPENS

The meeting had lasted over three hours, and people's patience with one another was wearing thin. There were still several items on the agenda, and I was looking at the clock, longing for closure. A short report on the recent General Conference of the denomination had just been given when the chair of the meeting asked for any comments. Suddenly, a woman jumped up without even being recognized. (Clearly, this was the moment she had been waiting for all night.) The denomination had been struggling with the inclusion of homosexuals in the life of the church, and the debate had made national headlines.

"I am sick and tired of the denomination taking such a liberal stance on issues that are incompatible with Christian teaching," she said. "We should protect ourselves. And since the denomination failed to do its job, we must decide this matter for ourselves right now! Homosexuality is clearly a sin, and there is no way we should accept anyone who is gay into membership. Certainly, we would not accept a gay pastor. We should also be clear that anyone who is gay will never be a leader in my church!" She went on for another fifteen minutes without allowing anyone to speak. With the passing of each moment, her voice was rising in pitch, callously condemning people and even suggesting at one point that the church should withdraw from the denomination over this matter. By now her emotions were in a high frenzy. People avoided looking at one another, and many wished they were anywhere else. Some, however, were nodding agreement. I was aware that there were several LGBTQ members of the church who were active in leadership. The chair gave into her outburst and was unable to bring the meeting to order. Chaos reigned. Finally she exploded: "I don't believe gay people are even Christians!" she shrieked. It was time for an intervention.

Whenever people come together, there is the possibility of conflict. You can try to run and hide, but you cannot escape conflict. It can happen anytime and anywhere. Religious institutions are not immune to it. People are not prepared to handle differences of opinion when they arise. They sit silently until tirades are over because they have learned that confronting people when they are out of control has not worked in the past. They simply became targets themselves and come under fire.

Most pastors have not been trained to handle conflict and therefore do not take the proper steps to prepare congregational leaders to handle disagreement before it gets out of control. The loudest voice in the room holds court over those gathered. Often congregations struggle with situations just like this one, hoping against hope that they will simply go away by themselves. They rarely do. Once words have been uttered, people begin to take sides or check out of the proceeding altogether. Churches have split or even discontinued over issues that were not handled properly. There was a small congregation in western Pennsylvania that actually voted to close because they did not know how to handle a bully that made every meeting a fight. Tired and frustrated, they simply gave up and gave the keys to the district superintendent!

Our society encourages combative decision-making. *Robert's Rules of Order* contributes to this by producing winners and losers and making issues and ideas right or wrong. We see confusion and paralysis in the American political system as well as on local levels. Conflict between nations often leads to war. When people act uncivilly toward one another someone gets hurt.

People must be taught how to interact with one another and make decisions in a healthy manner. They must be encouraged to bring their very best to the life of the church so that the congregation or religious group can provide a Christian witness to the world on how disciples in conflict behave. We must use approaches to conflict that are transformative.

There is a better way!

GOALS OF THIS CHAPTER

This chapter will help you

-define conflict and identify causes

-be a non-anxious presence and lead effectively

-effectively reduce tensions and heal relationships

-identify your natural conflict style and know when it is appropriate to use it

-learn six supports to transform conflict into a force for creativity and good

-provide a framework or process to resolve conflict in your ministry setting

-design a church behavioral guideline to guide members' actions

-seek common ground by developing good problem-solving techniques

-utilize good communication skills

WHAT IS CONFLICT?

Conflict is a situation in which two people or ideas are trying to occupy the same space at the same time. It is a disagreement or argument, typically, protracted where there is tension. It can test the resilience of a group.

We respond to conflict based on our own perspectives, assumptions, values, and cultures. If left unresolved, conflict can quickly get out of control. Eventually, unresolved conflict seeps into the fabric of the congregation and eventually destroys the goodwill of a group. People can no longer make good decisions or agree to disagree. When this happens, outside help is essential.

Your faith group is like a family with distinct personalities, behaviors, roles, patterns, and so on. These dynamics can lead to conflict when change occurs. Conflict can be

- within an individual
- between two individuals
- within a team or committee
- between two or more groups within an organization
- between the congregation and the community around it
- within a denomination

The way we approach conflict matters. We can choose to compete (view one another as adversaries and focus on differences) or collaborate (seek common ground and work together to creatively resolve an issue).

CONFLICT WARNING SIGNS

-There is no clear purpose or vision that guides decisions.

-Tradition becomes all powerful and change is avoided.

-Membership is declining and newcomers rarely stay.

-People in the pews are content to sit back and let others do the work.

-Giving is more of a duty than a joy in response to God's grace.

-People leave worship and meetings quickly rather than hang around to talk with one another.

-Differences lead to withdrawal; diversity is uncomfortable.

-Little laughter is heard.

What has been your experience? What have you noticed in your situation? What would you add to the list?

WHAT'S WORTH FIGHTING FOR?

For congregations the critical question is how to understand and participate in the mission of God. Churches have different ways of speaking about the mission of God. For example, The United Methodist Church (USA) speaks of "making disciples for the transformation of the world."

When members disagree on the purpose of the church and how to fulfill it there will be conflict. These are important conversations for the well-being of the church, and they deserve our best efforts to resolve them.

A valuable reference point when addressing such a conflict is to consider what needs to change in the church and what essentially needs to remain the same. Review the chart below to help you consider what is enduring and what can change without damaging the central tenets of a faith community. The first column remains the same; it is woven into the DNA of a congregation. The second column is how to live out the enduring qualities with integrity in a changed context.

ENDURING (FOUNDATIONAL)	CHANGING (SITUATIONAL)
Mission of the church (God-given)	Vision—how you will accomplish God's mission today
Values that are part of the church's DNA and guide behavior (go back to the formation of the congregation)	Methods—specifically the strategies and ministries you will use to accomplish vision
Principles and core beliefs (developed over time and shaped by life experiences)	Goals—those things you will accomplish during the coming year

Three congregations in Maine were yoked to share a pastor. The first thing that needed to be decided was when each church would gather for worship. Would it surprise you to know that they all wanted 11:00 a.m. on Sunday? It took the district superintendent three meetings with members to help them understand that worshipping God regularly was part of their core beliefs. That would not change. They did have an opportunity to ensure that worship happened with a variety of times and styles. How or when they worshipped could change and not destroy their core purpose. It was time for a new method. It took a lot of prayer to begin to look at the options: At first everyone wanted a Sunday morning time so it was determined the worship times would be 8:00 a.m., 9:30 a.m., and 11:00 a.m. to allow the pastor to travel among the congregations. Further, they were willing to rotate times quarterly so each church would meet at 11:00 a.m. part of the year. This became confusing for members of the community who often arrived at the wrong time and place because the church signs were not kept up to date. It became important to make a better decision. One church agreed to meet on Sunday at 9:00 a.m., another met at 11:00 a.m., and the third met at 5:00 p.m. The congregations accepted this arrangement because they could hold fast to what was enduring and important, that is, having worship, and by recognizing what could change: the time they would worship.

We waste time, resources, and energy chasing assumptions and groupthink. It takes courage to make healthy decisions that you can live with as a community of faith.

There are numerous signs that your church is making decisions in unhealthy ways:

- A matter has been decided yet stays on the agenda for frequent reconsideration, often leading to no action or complacency.

- People threaten one another if they do not get their way.

- The majority of the group remains silent during the discussion.

- Meetings called to make crucial decisions are poorly attended.

- People take things personally or attack one another over different perspectives or ideas.

- The pastor often spends valuable time trying to keep people happy and engaged in the process.

- People get their feelings hurt and stop coming to the church.

- Decisions are put off indefinitely rather than upset someone.

- There is frequent turnover in church staff and leadership.

BASIC PRINCIPLES REGARDING CONFLICT

-Conflict happens in the best of groups; it's a way of life.

-Conflict can occur whenever people gather to address an issue and make a decision.

-Churches must help their members deal well with conflict.

-Dealing well with conflict can be learned and practiced.

-Stress over how conflict is handled is one of the major reasons clergy and laity leave the church.

-We need one another to resolve conflict and make wise decisions.

-Conflict has advantages and disadvantages depending on how we deal with it.

-If handled well, conflict offers an opportunity and a blessing.

Think of a time when you experienced conflict in the church. What happened? Why does unresolved conflict cause so much harm?

COMMON CAUSES OF CONFLICT IN THE CHURCH

By raising an awareness of the causes of conflict, people can work through their differences with a greater sense of creativity and purpose. Review the list below and consider which ones you have observed.

1. CONFLICT OVER INTERPERSONAL RELATIONSHIPS

This type of conflict often occurs when there are strong emotions and poor communication present. It can also be triggered by negative behavior, imbalance in power, or competition.

    a.   games people play to get their way

    b.   unresolved grief from the past

    c.   lack of respect for one another

    d.   lack of trust and jealousy

    e.   low expectations of behavior (lack of boundaries)

    f.   lack of forgiveness and willingness to move on

2. CONFLICT OVER INFORMATION OR DATA

This type of conflict occurs when there is inadequate or false information present. It can also be caused by how facts are gathered, interpreted, or misunderstood.

    a.   poor communication skills

    b.   facts accidentally or intentionally distorted

    c.   assumptions made

    d.   lack of clarity around shared purpose

    e.   dishonesty

    f.   ignoring the facts to keep the peace

3. CONFLICT OVER ORGANIZATION, PROCESS, AND RESOURCES

This type of conflict arises when there is not a sound process to deal with tension or not enough time given to the task. A lack of boundaries often feeds the conflict. This conflict is often seen when there is little clarity on roles or tasks.

    a.   processes used to make decisions are counterproductive

    b.   triangulation rather than speaking to one another directly

    c.   lack of adequate time to deal with an issue

    d.   lack of a clear process and rules that everyone understands

    e.   poor preparation and no agenda with set times

    f.   illegal activity

4. CONFLICT OVER AUTHORITY AND INTERESTS

These conflicts occur when people's preferences are ignored. There can be hostility or suspicion toward leaders.

    a.   power struggles

    b.   failure to listen

    c.   forgotten history; unresolved previous conflict

d.   personal agendas allowed to take precedence over community choices

e.   denominational policies and practices differing from the local level

5. CONFLICT OVER VALUES AND GOALS

Conflicts in this category arise when the theology, purpose, or goals are threatened.

a.   church does not live out its stated values and purpose

b.   lack of commitment to transformative mission

c.   inability to welcome new people and ideas

d.   treatment of the church as personal property or turf protection

e.   differing perspectives within a group over the nature of God, role of Christian community, Christian values, lifestyle choices, and personal convictions

f.   lack of clarity on the criteria by which decions are made

g.   theological differences

Conflict can also be caused by a combination of these factors. Review these causes and determine the following:

*   What causes of conflict have you experienced?
*   Are there any causes harder for you to handle? Why?
*   Which causes are easier? Why?
*   How does knowing these causes of conflict help you resolve tensions?

BENEFITS OF CONFLICT

When handled properly, conflict

*   builds trust and confidence
*   restores relationships and makes them stronger

- deals decisively with an issue
- allows new insights and discoveries to be made
- energizes a group
- signals that people care about what is happening and that they are invested
- provides a powerful witness to others about how a Christian community can work together even in the midst of serious differences
- offers opportunities for growth

DISADVANTAGES OF CONFLICT

When mishandled, conflict

- destroys trust
- produces anger, hostility, and increased anxiety
- damages a sense of community and reputation
- wastes time and energy
- forces people to leave the church
- escalates tensions
- limits creative options

THE SEVEN LEVELS OF CONFLICT

There are seven basic levels of conflict. Each level requires its own strategies in order to resolve that conflict. Recognizing the level of conflict that you are dealing with helps you effectively address differences. A wrong response can make the situation worse.

Remember, when higher levels of conflict are present

- feelings will be more intense
- communication is challenged
- compromise is difficult

- there is more judgment and less compassion
- it takes longer to resolve matters

Review the following table for the seven levels of conflict and how to deal with them.

LEVEL	SIGNS	STRATEGIES
0. All is well (no conflict)	Goal: keeping the peace - Nothing is wrong - People are functioning at a high level of trust - Ministry is happening	- Monitor interactions between people
1. We have a problem to solve together (Misinformation)	Goal: solving a real problem - No personal attacks - High level of mutual respect and trust - Focus on the present - Language specific and supportive	- Define the problem - Share information - Search for options - Encourage collaboration and participation - Keep language focused on the facts
2. We disagree, but I want to look good (Strategies/Approach essential)	Goal: being right and saving face - Generalizations to talk about issues - Triangulating occurs - Trust suffers - Inaccuracies and mistakes pointed out - Records of wrongs kept - Cast doubts on the other's intent	- Seek to understand - Focus on common ground - Encourage expression of feelings - Rebuild trust - Ask clarifying questions - Stay in the moment
3. We're in a contest with one another and you must agree with me (Mutual goals not supported)	Goal: winning and getting your way - Power abused - Manipulation used - Hard to talk informally or laugh - People make cases on why they are right - Language becomes vague - Assumptions flourish - Personal attacks to influence - People take sides - "Us vs. Them" mentality reigns	- Agree on ground rules (not to attack the other and so on) - Use liturgical means: prayers of confession and pardon - Clarify assumptions and realities - Decide on a mutually agreeable goal(s) - Talk separately with the parties/leaders

4. We will protect ourselves; you must leave
 	
(norms and principles threatened)
	Goal: protecting the group by fighting or fleeing (factions emerge and organize)
	
	- Stereotypes voiced
	
	- Use of "you" statements rather than "I" statements
	
	- People Fight:
	
	  principles are at stake
	
	  no room for compromise
	
	- People Flee:
	
	  situation is hopeless—no resolution in sight
	
	  run away
	
	- Conflict shifts from issues to individuals
	
	- Attempt to expel people
	
	- Emotional attacks on the rise
	
	- Attempts made to get a third party to agree with you; might makes right
	
	- people are uncomfortable and panic
		- Separate the people from the issues
		
		- Identify dynamics
		
		- Surface majority view
		
		- Focus on problem
		
		- Identify boundaries
		
		- Mediate acceptable needs with top leaders not grass roots–level participation
		
		- Stress dangers of conflict at this level to the institution
		
		- Use good organization processes: votes, mediation, and so on
		
		- Allow people to leave with dignity

5. We're at war! (Core values under attack)	Goal: destroying the other (revenge) - People forget what started the conflict. Original goals are lost; issues become causes; ideologies create deep factions - People think the ends justify the means - One option pursued: destruction - People become avengers of truth and liberty and are unable to withdraw to get balance - Little language exchanged. - Positions deepen	- Hire a neutral arbitrator - Peace-keeping force or treaty is essential - Interim leadership helpful - Troublemakers must be disempowered or asked to leave - Stand down leadership for a specific period of time - Agree to separate or split
6. Mutual destruction	Organization is no longer viable	-Neutral representative of denomination liquidates assets -Harvest property for another use -Membership scatters

SIX STRATEGIES TO DECREASE CONFLICT

The best way to prevent conflict from getting out of control is to take preventative steps that can boost the immune system of the congregation. These strategies can turn conflict into cooperation.

SIX SUPPORTS TO RESOLVE CONFLICT

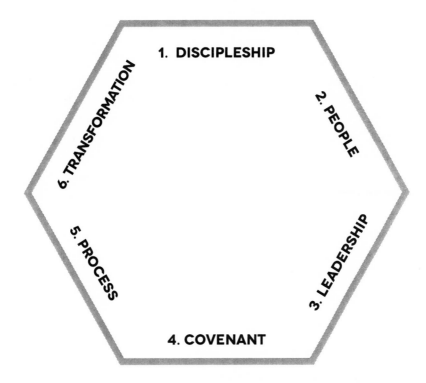

1. GROW IN YOUR DISCIPLESHIP

John Wesley, the founder of Methodism, talked about practicing the means of grace and the importance of immersing ourselves in those activities that help us grow as disciples. They are based on Christ's commandments to his disciples:

1. Love God with our whole being. These activities are known as "Vital Piety." These means of grace include participating in worship, Bible study, sacraments, prayer, fasting, singing hymns, and Christian conferencing.

2. Love your neighbor as well as you do yourself. These activities are known as "Acts of Compassion and Mercy" and include Matthew 25 ministries (feed the hungry, provide shelter and clothing, visit people in need, and so on). John Wesley added two additional emphases: seek the common good and make peace.

Congregations that immerse themselves in these practices tend to be more resilient in the midst of conflict. It is often helpful to begin gatherings by lighting the Christ Candle to remind people that God is in their midst and should be considered in their thoughts, actions, and decisions as well. In addition, these activities can help refocus a group away from the needs of individuals to attend to the needs of the community: deep prayer, devotions, and Bible or book studies. When a serious conflict is resolved, many congregations find it very helpful to hold a Service of Healing and Reconciliation including anointing people with liturgy to move forward together.

When people are actively growing as disciples of Jesus Christ and trying to discern the will of God together, they are less likely to get into a pattern of fighting. By allowing scripture and theology to reshape us, we can correct our perspective, which is often the cause of conflict. Spiritual practices renew our hearts and can revive a fresh perspective in a faith community.

Being a believer of Jesus Christ changes the way we see ourselves, one another, and the world around us. Jesus commanded us to love one another (John 13:34-35). When we love one another, we

- center our lives in Christ
- honor and respect one another
- live in peace with one another
- bear with one another
- serve one another
- encourage one another
- build one another up

Even when we disagree we are called to be ambassadors of Christ and reconcile ourselves to the call of Christ. Galatians 5:22-23 reminds us that when we live in Christ we have the fruit of the spirit (peace, patience, love, etc.). These things make it possible for us to forgive one another and move beyond conflict. Matthew 23:34, Romans 14:17, and 2 Corinthians 5:16-20 offer more lessons about reconciliation and forgiveness. How grounded in scripture are your leaders? How do members of the congregation practice all the means of grace? What evidence do you have that people are clear about the purpose of the church and what it means to live as disciples of Jesus Christ?

2. VALUE THE PERSON

When engaging in a conflicted situation a person's emphasis on either tasks or relationships will be a major factor in how that person responds. Different situations may warrant different approaches; however, healthy communities and effective decisions will be achieved when people in conflict value relationships as highly as tasks. Therefore, understanding one another is crucial.

Know Your Conflict Style

Each of us has a distinct style of response that guides how we interact with others when in conflict. Understanding ourselves and one another is crucial in fostering the awareness necessary to prevent conflict from escalating out of control. Learning and respecting the gifts that we each contribute to interactions are essential.

Consider these conflict styles to learn the five styles that are present among group members when they are trying to work through conflict. How do you typically react in a conflicted situation? If given a choice, do you prefer to reach a goal or maintain relationships? There are people who are more task-oriented and prefer just to get the job done. Their focus is on completing the work. Others are more relational and prefer to take into account the feelings of others when making decisions. There are also people who prefer to focus on the task and to value relationships while doing it.

There are many ways to respond to conflict. Kenneth W. Thomas and Ralph H. Kilmann introduced their Thomas–Kilmann Conflict Mode Instrument (TKI) in 1974. It has quickly become the best-known conflict style inventory.[1]

1. Avoiding: We Both Lose

People who respond in this way tend to work through conflict by backing off and withdrawing when conflict occurs. They prefer not to deal with an issue that disturbs the peace. They prefer to be calm and silent in a situation. This strategy can be helpful when people need a timeout so conflict does not escalate, when matters are trivial, or when the preservation of the status quo

---

1. Consulting Psychological Press holds the copyright to this thirty-question questionnaire to determine your conflict style.

is more important than relationships or resolution. When not used wisely this style saps energy and can leave a residue of negative feelings and a loss of accountability.

2. Competing: I Win/You Lose

People who respond in this way tend to work through conflict by bringing others around to their point of view. It tends to be a "my-way-or-no-way" approach. This style is most effective when you need to make quick decisions, preserve important values, and protect those unable to protect themselves. However, when misused, this style can destroy relationships and lead to a loss of cooperation, anger, depression, broken relationships, and diminished respect.

3. Compromising: Win Some/Lose Some

People who respond this way prefer to negotiate to find common ground where the issue and relationships are equally important. They believe the middle ground is best and prefer solutions that are acceptable to each party. This style is most effective when it is possible to give and take for the good of the group. When misused, this style often leaves everyone dissatisfied and fails to implement the optimal decision.

4. Accommodating: I Lose/You Win

People who respond this way like to agree with others and often use appeasement and flattery to get through conflict. They like everyone to get along and be happy and will sacrifice their needs and feelings for the good of the group. This style is effective when the decision is not a big deal or when relationships matter the most and the harmony of the group is at stake. When misused, it causes the power to shift to one group or viewpoint and can make it difficult to creatively resolve matters by limiting dialogue and information sharing.

5. Collaborating: I Win/You Win

People who respond this way are keen to have conversation on how both the issue and the relationship matter. When used effectively, this style gathers information, explores alternatives, encourages dialogue, uses process well, is open to change, and welcomes disagreement. It requires a significant amount of time and hard work for this style to succeed because it requires maturity and understanding of healthy confrontation.

Personalities

Each of us is born with various gifts and abilities. Your personality is hardwired into your being and guides the way you get energized, receive information, make decisions, and organize your world. In every group there are a variety of personalities. They can be a blessing if understood or a curse if ignored.

Carl Jung, a Swiss psychiatrist, developed a theory of personality and explained how people are unique. Isabel Myers and her mother, Catherine Briggs, discovered Jung's work after years of observing people and coming to the same conclusion. They designed the Myers-Briggs Type Indicator (MBTI)[2] for people to learn their personality.

Here is a brief overview of the MBTI and conflict. Note that the MBTI points out behaviors that surface in times of conflict and create difficulties in communication.

BRIEF OVERVIEW OF THE MYERS-BRIGGS TYPE INDICATOR

SOURCE OF ENERGY

EXTROVERSION (E)	INTROVERSION (I)
Energized by external or social world	Energized by internal world of experience and thoughts
Speak their minds easily	Reflect before speaking
May not listen carefully; are eager to express themselves	May not say enough; regret a missed opportunity to express themselves
Talk loud and fast	Like advance notice on issues and time to prepare
Prefer to talk out problems now and get frustrated when this is not possible	May withdraw inside themselves when conflict occurs

---

2. Myers-Briggs Type Indicator (Gainesville, FL: Consulting Psychologist Press, 2016), tel. 800.624.1765.

RECEIVE INFORMATION

SENSING (S)	INTUITION (N)
Gather information using their five senses to observe things	Gather information through intuition, possibilities, and undercurrents
Like to argue the facts and may miss what lies behind the words	Tend to make broad generalizations and rush to see patterns
Can get lost in the irrelevant details and miss the bigger issue	May miss the obvious or forget inconvenient details
Concerned for injustice	Concerned for grace

PROCESS INFORMATION (WHERE PEOPLE PREFER TO FOCUS THEIR ATTENTION IN CONFLICT)

THINKING (T)	FEELING (F)
Preference for logic, deduction, and rational objectivity	Preference for a subjective response based on values, emotions, and so on
Tend to get to analytical and task focused	Tend to accept and appreciate differences
Have succinct delivery when addressing conflict; concern for objective data	Have tactful delivery when addressing conflict; concern about the impact on others
Maintain a firm position in attempting to resolve conflict; may seem cold	Ensure there is give and take in resolving conflict; may seem too emotional

MAKES DECISIONS AND ACTS (CAUSES THE GREATEST TENSION BETWEEN PEOPLE)

JUDGING (J) – ORGANIZING OUR WORLD	PERCEIVING (P) – LIVING SPONTANEOUSLY
Make decisions quickly; tend to reach conclusions before considering all options	Like to take their time making a decision; can see all sides of an issue
Sort out the details well; view things as right or wrong	Seek clarification; may overcomplicate an issue and lose momentum
Focus on present and future and plan accordingly	Focus on the present and not give due consideration to time pressures
Concern for output or outcome of situation	Concern for input of participants

You do not need everyone in your congregation to take a MBTI to understand how type affects communication and conflict. Here are some tips for using type in resolving conflict:

- Consider offering a type workshop in your organization.

- Use type as a way to understand differences and similarities and how the different approaches that they bring is helpful to making good decisions.

- Explain type as a way to see the strengths of your organization.

- Affirm the contribution of all types and how necessary it is to listen to others.

- Plan agendas and tasks so that type is recognized and explored as you work through issues.

- Be aware of your own type and that how you may prefer to work may not work for everyone.

3. HONOR YOUR LEADERSHIP ROLE

Remember the story in Exodus of Moses and his exhaustion? Moses was trying to be all and do all while becoming less effective. His father-in-law, Jethro, reminded him that he had available to him the gifts and abilities of others to share the workload. When Moses focused on taking care of himself and focusing on his main task, things became easier. Instead of having a dependent people, the Israelites became interdependent upon one another.

As you consider your role as pastor or lay leader, do you try to do too much and unintentionally reject the abilities or views of others? How do you develop a team of people working with you that function with a high level of trust and respect?

It is your task as a leader to keep your organization on the track of dealing with issues before they get out of control. Consider these tips as you lead in conflict situations:

- Stop avoiding conflict; address issues in a timely manner.

- Learn how to "care front" unhelpful behavior without embarrassing people.

- Remain a nonanxious presence in the midst of conflict; stay calm.

- Own your feelings and beliefs; don't take things personally.

- Assure a fair process.

- Maintain boundaries.

33

- Be proactive rather than reactive. Give yourself time to think and speak wisely.
- Establish a high level of trust.
- Don't take sides.
- Seek reconciliation and healing.
- Know when to ask for help and name your limitations.
- Foster good communication:
    - Provide a safe environment for people to work through their differences.
    - Address issues in a transparent and direct manner.
    - Be hard on the issues yet soft on people.
    - Use "I" rather than "you" statements.
    - Call a "timeout" when things get hot.
    - When necessary, apologize.
    - Invite people to talk out issues and feelings.

What would you add to this list?

4. ESTABLISH A BEHAVIORAL COVENANT

Successfully developing a behavioral covenant involves

- gathering as many members of the group as possible
- encouraging an open and transparent process
- generating a list of values from the Bible and other sources that the group believes should guide their life together, that is, respect, listening, and so on
- providing the list to a drafting group to prepare a one-page covenant in which the values are expressed positively (e.g., "We will...")

A behavioral covenant needs to be owned by the leadership and members. Therefore the draft covenant needs to be circulated and adopted for use. Covenants are effective when they are integrated into the life of a group. So they should be taught about, prominently displayed, promoted, included in orientation of leaders and membership classes, and be regularly reviewed. For an example of a covenant Google "Christian Behavioral Covenant."

5. WORK THROUGH A PROCESS

An important scripture that guides the interactions of Christians in conflict is found in Matthew 18:15-20:

> If your brother or sister sins against you, go and correct them when you are alone together. If they listen to you, then you've won over your brother or sister. But if they won't listen, take with you one or two others so that every word may be established by the mouth of two or three witnesses. But if they still won't pay attention, report it to the church. If they won't pay attention even to the church, treat them as you would a Gentile and tax collector. I assure you that whatever you fasten on earth will be fastened in heaven. And whatever you loosen on earth will be loosened in heaven. Again I assure you that if two of you agree on earth about anything you ask, then my Father who is in heaven will do it for you. For where two or three are gathered in my name, I'm there with them.

This passage helps us work through our differences with one another. When two people find themselves in disagreement, this scripture provides a framework to work through it and be reconciled. Matthew 18 reminds us to do several things:

- In the spirit of humility, meet with one another and try to work out differences directly in private. Seek forgiveness and reconciliation. Do not triangulate the matter by talking to others!

- If this does not resolve matters, the parties are invited to meet with two to three people whom they trust who will listen to their situation and offer feedback on how to resolve the matters in a just manner. This should be a confidential meeting.

- If the previous steps have failed, the individuals need to decide if the matter is serious enough to warrant further external support. In this case it could be brought before the church council or an appropriate committee. This group listens to each person and decides how the parties will resolve their differences.

6. AIM FOR TRANSFORMATION

Ultimately, we do not want to simply resolve contentious issues; we want to grow and be transformed through the experience of them. William Bridges wrote a powerful book: *Manage Transitions—Making the Most Out of Change*.[3] It is a must-read for leaders in the midst of change.

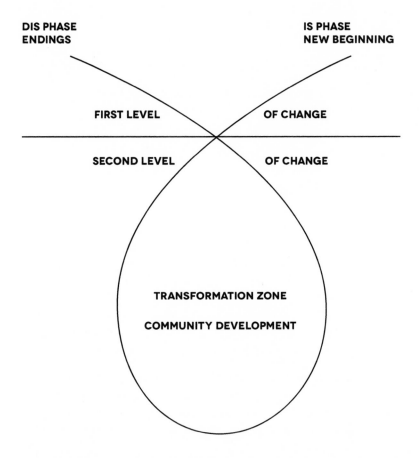

This diagram explains how change can come from conflict. This DIS Phase is a place where people sense things are coming to an end or about

---

3. William Bridges, *Manage Transitions—Making the Most Out of Change* (Boston: Da Capo Lifelong, 2009).

to change. Think about what happens when people know that there will be a change of a pastor. Once people know that their pastor is about to move, they may become dis-engaged, dis-organized, dis-identified, and dis-enchanted with the pastor and even the church. This is the part of the cycle during which conflict may surface. If you simply try to make people happy or gloss things over, your congregation becomes stuck, and the conflict can simmer for years. The IS phase is a place of new beginnings. People are ready to identify with the ministries of the church, engage in new opportunities for service, organize for growth, and recommit to the congregation again.

Moving from the DIS phase to the IS phase never works. Glossing over conflict and getting people to get along without dealing with the issues only deal with the first order of change (surface issues). The consequence of first order of change is that things will still surface and require more effort and energy later. When this happens, congregations have the same fights over and over again.

For conflict to be transformative, the deep work of second-level change is required. This means going beneath the surface and spiritually shaping the community of faith. We are changing who we are and how we do things in light of scripture, experience, reason, and tradition. This is holy and vital work if a congregation or group is to be healthy.

The transformation zone is the place where you

- select a process to address conflict

- attend to the means of grace

- attend to relationships, celebrating people's unique personalities and abilities

- remember and affirm your mission and core values

- train people and give them the skills necessary to deal with conflict

- surface options for addressing issues

- provide a safe environment/process that allows people to work through conflict or differences with a fresh perspective

- provide pertinent information about the issue in contention

- work on reconciliation and healing

- revise leadership tasks and responsibilities
- foster good communication (open and transparent)
- document your decision or agreement
- hold a Service of Reconciliation and Healing and anoint people at its close

Only after you have taken the time to work through the transformation cycle is it possible to have a new beginning and celebrate renewal. Yes, this takes time to do well!

CONCLUSION

Do you remember the case study from the beginning of the chapter about an irate woman in the church council meeting who thought that homosexuality was sin and that LGBTQ individuals should not hold leadership in her church? The story moved from confrontation to collaboration.

Finally, she paused to take a breath when a quiet voice came from the back of the room spoke: "Mom, do you mean me?" It was her son, Sam, who had spoken up. The room grew very still waiting for her response as she realized that the people she had been criticizing a moment ago now included her only child whom she loved dearly. It became apparent that she had no idea that he was gay! What happened next was a miracle. "Forgive me, Son. I love you and obviously have some things to learn about being a Christian. I need your help." Then she turned to the group and asked for their prayers and patience. She asked the pastor and staff to plan a conversation about the issue of sexuality in the church and give some guidance on how they should treat one another. Her son seconded the matter, and healing slowly began. Today the congregation is a reconciling place of welcome and inclusion for all people without discrimination in the wider community.

In the Philippines there is a word: *Bayanihan*. It means a communal effort to achieve a shared goal. It also refers to the practice of a group moving a house to a location where a new family will dwell. So it takes all of us working together to move God's house though conflict to be in the place where God calls us to be active in the world. Resolving conflict well enables us to accomplish God's mission.

REFLECTION QUESTIONS

1. What did you learn about your attitude to conflict and your leadership style in it?

2. How has your congregation or ministry setting typically addressed conflict?

3. Review the Six Supports to Resolve Conflict (Discipleship, People, Leadership, Covenant, Process, and Transformation), which of them do you need to strengthen in order to be a more effective leader in conflict situations?

4. Have you identified any new strategies that you can apply in your ministry context? What are they?

ACTIVITY

1. Think about a recent conflict in your ministry settings. Describe it:

    _____

    _____

    _____

    _____

    _____

2. For this stressful situation, answer the following questions:

    a. What happened? How did it start?

    b. What did you say or do in response? How did you contribute to the conflict?

    c. How did the other person(s) react?

    d. How did the encounter leave you feeling?

3. If you could turn back time and relive these moments, what different words or actions would have changed the outcome for the better?

4. When conflict occurs, identify the patterns or behaviors you naturally make (fight, flight, withdrawal, be defensive, and so on).

5. Identify one of these behaviors to modify and improve so stressful situations do not turn into battles.

VALUES THAT ENHANCE FAITHFUL DECISION-MAKING

WHAT DO YOU THINK YOU ARE DOING?

There is a story told of a man walking beside a large building site in a town during medieval times. The place was a hive of activity with many people working on the site as a new structure slowly rose out of the ground.

As the traveler passed alongside the workmen, he saw one smashing rocks with a large hammer in a desultory manner, cursing with every downbeat of his sledgehammer. Clearly the worker was miserable, and so the traveler asked the man what was the problem. The gruff reply came: "How would you feel if you had to smash rocks day after day in the blazing sun?" Further down the road was another man equally as miserable as he sought to reduce a pile of rocks to gravel. "What are you doing, sir?" asked the interested pilgrim. The man replied "I am trying to feed my family by turning big rocks into little rocks so the builders can drop them into that hole over there where no one will ever see them again!"

Finally, the traveler came to a third man who had the largest pile of rocks next to him. This man was sweating and tired but sang and smiled as he swung the heavy hammer time after time. "And what makes you so happy while you work at this difficult task?" he asked. "Oh sir," the man replied with joy, "I am laying the foundation for a wonderful cathedral that will stand tall for centuries and will allow all who worship in it to sing praises to God and to have their lives blessed!"

There is a saying that beauty is in the eye of the beholder. It is also the case that when people see value in what they are doing, they behave differently to those who see their work as less valuable. Looking at our work in a certain way—a way that takes in the big picture—affects the way we go about our business. Only attitude separated the three workers doing the same task.

Can you think of occasions when the way that you have looked at a task affected the way that you approached it? Has your perspective affected your emotions around your work? Has your viewpoint given you a sincere desire to be involved? Has your viewpoint affected the way you relate to others who are also involved in the task? That has certainly been our experience in so many areas of life.

How we behave in a particular context is profoundly affected by the attitudes that we bring to the situation. We have been to church meetings that have been hard work to attend and that we have regarded as having little value. In those settings we have just gone through the motions until the arduous task was over. Alternatively we are sure that many of us have been to church meetings that are just part of the job. This is a common risk for people who serve as pastors or other professionals in the life of the church. They think that church meetings are just part of the job and want to get them done even if they think no one will ever see the results of all their hard work. Yet on some occasions we have been energized and uplifted as we have realized that in this ordinary meeting of the people of God, we are caught up in an activity that will be a blessing to others and that will have lasting effects long after our little piece of the project has finished.

When Christians meet to make decisions, the perspective that they have on what they are doing has a profound effect on their attitudes, relationships, and behavior. Having a positive and healthy understanding of what it is you are doing always makes a huge difference, and the value of church meetings is no different.

No one reading this book will be naive enough to believe that everyone coming to a church meeting arrives with the same motives. Quite likely there will be the bored, the obliged, and the hopeful all in the same meeting. In addition, it will often be the case that people are arriving at a meeting with different preconceived agendas and goals that are set in concrete before the chair even calls the meeting to order. When people arrive with all these different attitudes and motives, then it is no wonder that church meetings can witness a display of many different attitudes, emotions, and practices. Each attitude, emotion, and practice will be consistent with where the people are coming from as they participate in the meeting. The trouble is that these attitudes, emotions, and practices will often work at cross-purposes to one another. In some situations they lead to very negative experiences and a stalemate in getting to a decision.

It is impossible to overstate the importance of having an agreed purpose for every aspect of church life. Many books have been written about the importance of a common vision for shaping the practices of a congregation, how church boards or entities are better able to marshal their resources by having a clear mission, and how individual Christians who have a clear sense of their ministry or vocation can be more consistent in their learning goals and application of their gifts. This book makes the case that it is equally important when congregations, church boards, districts, presbyteries, synods, or conferences meet that they have an agreed understanding of their purpose. When there is an agreed understanding of the purpose then meeting practices and processes will be put in place, which support that understanding. Alignment of practices with an agreed purpose is always a good thing to do!

WHERE WE ARE TODAY

Perhaps once it may have been possible to talk about denominations having a common understanding on most issues. In the formation period for churches there were usually very particular issues that shaped their character and values. Frequently, these hallmarks of a church's tradition were born out of conflict. So when people chose to be Methodist, Presbyterian, Baptist, Pentecostal, Congregational, and so on, they knew that they were joining people of a like mind around issues that were of great importance to them and their community of faith. In the early years of new churches there is always a common narrative that makes sense of who the people are and what is expected of them.

Without fail, this narrative or framework of belief includes an agreed understanding of how decisions will be made, that is, where authority rests in the particular faith community. In church language we talk about this as the polity of the church or the way things are governed.

All polity is theologically grounded whether or not most members of the church recognize this. Church government, or polity, is the practical outworking of significant theological positions. Polity has embedded within it certain assumptions about

- the way power is exercised
- who has power
- how the will of God is mediated to the community of faith
- the practices and processes that support faithful decision making

Do you know your denomination's foundational story? Do you know what the theological convictions are that undergird the polity of your church? Do you know what your way of doing church business says about power and authority, where it rests in the church, how the will of God is mediated to the community of faith and the processes and practices that support faithful Christian decision-making? Do the other members of your congregation, church council, board, district, synod, or conference hold to the same understandings? This is important. If different theological views are held on these matters, do you think that it might affect the way that people operate in church meetings? If there is a significant difference of opinion on these crucial theological issues, then the chances are very high that there will be conflict in your meetings and decisions.

If once it could be said that there was a meta-narrative or framework of belief that was shared by members of major denominations, then this is no longer the case. Today church members are divided over theological, ethical, moral, and polity issues that once were agreed (or, at least, taken for granted). The breakdown of the denominational meta-narrative as the basis for unity is having profound effects across the life of many Christian churches and is at the core of the many conflicts that are tearing denominations and congregations apart. It is important for the church to have a discussion about how unity is sustained in the face of the collapse of the denominational frameworks that defined and sustained unity. However, that is not the purpose of this book. The point to make here is that the theological positions that have made the polity of a church something on which there was widespread agreement are unraveling, just as much as the other theological underpinnings of unity. Consequently, it can no longer be taken for granted that when Christians meet together to make decisions that they all understand the project in the same way.

WHAT IS THE PURPOSE OF CHURCH BUSINESS MEETINGS?

As you think about some of the church meetings that you attend, what do you think people attending think is the purpose of the meeting? As we have tried to understand what is going on when people behave in a particular way in church meetings, this is the list that we come up with. You may develop a different list to this one, which is fine. As you read the list you will see that they are not all mutually exclusive, and so people may hold more than one of these positions at the same time. The list talks about what people do, what it says about their understanding of the purpose for meeting, and some of the theological assumptions that undergird or justify that position.

EXAMPLE 1: THE SOURCE OF POWER

Behavior:	People arrive at the meeting closed-minded and determined to get their way on an issue.
Understanding:	Meetings are places where power is exercised in order to get things done (or stopped).
Theology:	Discerning the will of God happens when like-minded people get together and come to a view on a subject. The church, through decisions in its meetings, can compel compliance with the will of God as that has been determined by a special/privileged/elite group prior to discussion with the whole community of faith.

EXAMPLE 2: A NECESSARY EVIL

Behavior:	Leaders/committees arrive with a well-developed position. If there is debate, it is controlled and dissent is not encouraged.
Understanding:	Meetings are necessary evils because they must be used to authorize actions; and participants are generally considered to be uninformed and unable to make complex decisions.
Theology:	Leaders are graced by God to lead and should be allowed to do that without unnecessary interference.

EXAMPLE 3: THE LEGISLATURE/PARLIAMENT

Behavior:	Participants regularly advocate for the views of people who are not in the meeting.
Understanding:	Meeting attenders are delegates for other groups or key individuals. Meetings are like parliaments in which the people who elect the attenders/delegates expect that their points of view will be presented and delegates don't have scope for independent action.
Theology:	The church is a democracy and not a theocracy, so the meeting goers have no independence to offer leadership, because the majority should get their way.

EXAMPLE 4: COMPLIANCE

Behavior:	One or two individuals seek to dominate the group through a variety of strategies in order to get their way. Other participants acquiesce to the pressure and suppress the expression of alternative points of view.
Understanding:	Meetings are just another context in which the patriarch/matriarch/power block controls the organization. Keeping the peace is more important than the decisions that are taken.
Theology:	The church is a vehicle for the advancement of personal positions. Position or status is privileged in the purposes of God.

EXAMPLE 5: THE SUPPORT GROUP

Behavior:	Leaders bring decisions that have already been made and introduce them to the wider group. While there may be scope for questions, there is no real attempt to open up the decision for amendment. A similar pattern is where an idea for a proposed direction is brought by the leader and feedback is solicited from the wider group before the decision is taken later by the leader.
Understanding:	The meeting is a context in which the leader seeks to bring the group along with decisions that have already been taken; or it is used as a sounding board for developing ideas. The meeting is used to build support for, or to road test, ideas that are generated elsewhere.
Theology:	Leadership and authority are vested in the same place. This is usually in an individual, such as the senior pastor, or a small leadership group that is understood to be called (sometimes said to be anointed) by God for leadership. The members are there to do the work of the church, the will of God, by following the leader who God has put in authority over them and not to exercise authority themselves.

EXAMPLE 6: COMMUNITY-BASED DISCERNMENT

Behavior:	All people present are encouraged and empowered to participate. The views of all are taken into account as new insights are developed, and consensus is built in the discernment of a common mind.
Understanding:	A group of people is the context in which it is most likely that the will of God will be discerned. Everyone present has a contribution to make and is needed. The meeting has authority (as defined in its rules) to act on behalf of the whole organization.
Theology:	Discernment is a group task undertaken by the people called and gifted by the Holy Spirit to offer leadership in this way. God is able to mediate God's will for the church through such a process. The church is a theocracy and not a democracy.

If you do this exercise with a group of leaders, hopefully it will be clear to you how different practices in meetings clearly indicate the views that people have about the nature and purpose of a church meeting. These views can be assessed sociologically, culturally, psychologically, politically, and no doubt in other ways, too. These can be very helpful processes of analysis. Even so, we are encouraging you to analyze the views that people hold about meetings from a theological perspective.

Theology is the language of the Christian faith. Theology seeks to locate what we do and believe within the tradition of the scriptures and the historic understandings of the church. When we articulate our positions theologically then they can be critiqued by the scriptures, tradition, and the experience of the church throughout the centuries. However, when we do not do the theological work then we are left to try and address our different points of view through the prism of politics, economics, sociology, or psychology.

We encourage you in your particular context to talk together about what you think you are doing when you meet as a group of Christians to make decisions. Check for consistency between the behaviors that people demonstrate and the underlying theology that these actions stand upon and affirm. Talk together about why the members of your group think that some theological positions are worthy of support and others are not.

CHRISTIAN TRADITIONS ABOUT MEETINGS

There are many theological traditions about leadership and how a Christian community discerns the will of God. This book does not denigrate different theological understandings of how leadership and authority are exercised in different parts of the church.

Within the Christian traditions from which the authors come, the historic and generally agreed theological position is that Christians meeting together, prepared by the appropriate spiritual disciplines, are the way in which the will of God for a community of faith is most likely to be discerned. Protestant traditions are generally tentative about claiming too much for themselves when it comes to knowing the mind of God. However, there is a very strong and confident tradition in which the best chance of discerning the will of God is when that project is undertaken as a corporate activity, in which the views of all participants are taken into account, and in which the community comes with openness to the leading of the Holy Spirit.

Methodism has a very strong and well-developed tradition of corporate decision-making. The language of conferencing in congregations, districts, and annual conferences affirms at every point of the church's decision-making life that discernment is a corporate activity. Wesley exhorted his followers to conference together so that they would know what to teach and what to do. Wesley exhorted that preparation for conferencing include prayer, meditation on the scriptures, doing acts of mercy and kindness, and partaking of Holy Communion. When these preparations had been undertaken, Wesley considered that the people were prepared for a process of conferencing, which makes it possible for them to discern what God would have them teach and do.

The Presbyterian Church is named after the foundational element of its form of church government—the Presbytery. The Presbytery is a council that functions as the corporate bishop, providing encouragement, guidance, and oversight to the ministers and congregations within its bounds. In local congregations, a group of lay persons (called elders), with the ordained minister, exercises government on behalf of the church in a group known as the Session. The minister is referred to as the teaching elder and as such shares leadership with the other elders in yet another example of community-based or corporate decision-making.

Congregational-based polities are self-evidently premised on the view that it is through a process of group deliberation that God is able to lead the community of faith in its obedience.

It is possible to go wider than these traditions and find other affirmations about the value and efficacy of community-based discernment processes. One of the most significant of these other traditions is the Religious Society of Friends (the Quakers). This spiritually focused Christian community has sustained a very healthy and faithful set of attitudes and practices that supports community-based discernment. Many of the principles that this book advocates can be found in writings about the Christian character and spiritual practices that undergird Quaker meeting procedures.[1]

At the heart of all these traditions is the theological conviction that when Christians meet to do the business of the church, this group of people is meeting to discern the will of God for this community. This is a high calling. It is an understanding of the role of a church meeting, which leads to very specific attitudes and practices in the participants. Or put alternatively, if the purpose of our congregational, board, regional, national, and international meetings is to discern the will of God for a particular Christian group in a certain place and time, then this will demand of the people who participate in these meetings that they take up certain attitudes and behave in certain ways.

As noted above, the primary theological affirmation is that it is in a community of mutual accountability that Christians are most likely to find the faithful way. The necessary corollary of this is that it must be possible for God to mediate God's will to this group of people; they are not left to their own wisdom and resources. The means through which God leads God's people include the following:

- the scriptures, prayer, and worship including Holy Communion
- tradition
- reason and experience
- the prophetic voice in the group
- a growing sense of agreement about the right course of action

---

1. Eden Grace, "An Introduction to Quaker Business Practice," http://www.edengrace .org/quakerbusiness.html.

Another important theological foundation for a consensus-building approach to discernment is that leadership can come from anyone in the group. Leadership and authority are not the same thing. In 2 Samuel, a story is told about the prophet Nathan who participated in the court of King David (12:1-7a). David clearly had the authority. He was the king, anointed by God to rule. But the person with authority had strayed from the will of God. Leadership was required so God raised up the prophet Nathan to give leadership to the one in authority. At the end of the day it would be for David to decide whether to accept this leadership or reject it. However, the importance of recognizing that leadership does not always come from those in authority is well made here. It is important for churches to leave spaces where the leadership that God wants to give can come from outside the power systems of the church.

When people gather for a process of Christian discernment, they are called and equipped by God for this high calling. The people who are in attendance are able to understand the issues and to make a contribution to the process. Church business meetings are not just for the people who we think have the expertise to be involved; it is for the people God wants to have involved. Where church members are appointed to the church's decision-making body, they should be respected as part of God's gift to that discernment process. Accordingly all participants should be supported to be involved to the fullest extent possible.

ATTITUDES AND PRACTICES THAT EXPRESS THESE THEOLOGICAL POSITIONS

These theological convictions lead to understandings about the attitudes and practices that should be present among the people who are using a consensus-building approach to discernment.

ATTITUDES

1. Openness toward God

Participants enter into the process expecting to be led by the Holy Spirit. People come conscious of their immense privilege to be working with God to deliver God's hopes and dreams for this community of faith. This is a high calling, and people are constantly listening for the leading of the Holy Spirit.

2. Vulnerability

People become open to the real possibility that the meeting will go a different direction to the one that was their first idea about the best way forward. Certainly they do not come with predetermined positions or as spokespersons for others, for which they will advocate come what may.

People will come with the operating assumption that they cannot know the will of God on their own and will therefore expect that something new will develop during the course of the process. They will examine themselves and their motives to see what it is that prevents them from being willing or able to change. People will be spiritually prepared to hear the surprising unexpected voice of the lonely prophet. They will protect the prophet in the court of the king (2 Samuel 12:1-7).

3. Respect

Communities can only genuinely exist when people appreciate, care for, and support one another. Unless the people who meet together to discern the will of God are caring and supportive of one another—even when they are in disagreement—then they cannot be a community. If they are not a community, then they cannot do community-based discernment. Valuing each and every member of the group is indispensable to effective community-based discernment.

4. Patience

Respecting people means that patience is required. Listening to every point of view and making sure that everyone has had a chance to understand and be involved takes time. Concern for the quality of the community's life and the well-being of its members takes precedence over getting through the agenda.

People matter more than resolutions because the people, the community, are the prerequisites for getting the decisions that align with the will of God.

5. Humility

No one owns the work of discernment; it belongs to the community. Everything is offered in hope of its usefulness but without seeking to possess and control what becomes of it. People recognize the limits of their wisdom and celebrate the contributions of others. When insights, experiences, and thoughts that are different to their own are offered, they resist the temptation to validate them by running them through the sieve of their own experiences and viewpoints. Rather these offerings are thankfully received as a gift from God.

6. Trust

People arrive at the meeting with the attitude that everyone is on the same side. People are trusted to be collaborators. Where the actions of some do not seem to reflect this same understanding, then those people are challenged and called out to behave in a way that is true to the purpose of the meeting. Trust needs to be expected, built, confirmed, and exhibited. Trust that we are all on the same side—the side of discerning the will of God for this community in this place and time—should be the normative attitude of all participants.

7. Transparency

People don't play games. They are honest about what they are trying to achieve, open about their motives, and clear about the processes in which they are engaged. They do not keep secrets or seek to manipulate the outcome through political maneuvering. A commitment to, and practice of, transparency is essential if the members of the group are going to be respected and supported in making their contribution to discernment.

PRACTICES

1. Worship and Spiritual Disciplines

Church business meetings go for differing lengths of time. Whatever the length of a church meeting it is essential that people participate in them prayerfully, informed by the scriptures and spiritually prepared and resourced.

Longer meetings may include more formal worship activities, and this is to be encouraged in addition to the times when people are called aside for prayer and reflection, which can occur in any meeting at any time.

Notwithstanding that meetings may be relatively short, prayer, scripture, and worship should be prominent parts of these gatherings, too. They serve to remind people of why they are there and whose purposes they serve. However, the good news is that God does not only prepare and resource people for meetings after the chair calls the meeting to order! People can be encouraged to make the agenda of a meeting a matter for prayer and a basis for scriptural reflection long before they arrive. Churches would do well to provide their members with resources that help them to undertake spiritual preparation before they arrive at business meetings.

2. Building Community

Relationships don't just happen. Relationships need to be encouraged, nurtured, and supported. When meetings are held with the same people each time, it is possible to overlook the need to gather this community of people together. People bring all sorts of joys and concerns with them to a meeting. They have left things behind to attend. Helping people share these— or other—things builds deeper relationships and enhances the capacity of people to listen, respect, and care for one another in a discernment process.

When church meetings are temporary communities made up of many people who are strangers to one another, it is imperative that time be taken in community-building. Methodologies include sharing around a meeting table using simple ice-breaker questions, using social opportunities at an event to get people to mix and meet, encouraging people to sit with people they do not already know, and using community groups for deeper engagement with one another.

3. Listening Long and Carefully to Everyone

Establishing well-thought-out and structured ways of listening is the key to showing respect and to creating a context in which the attitudes of humility and vulnerability can be fostered.

Listening can be facilitated in a wide variety of ways. Small-group discussions can be a very powerful way to assist those who are shy or are slower at developing and articulating their thoughts, or are less confident in speaking

English, or are not comfortable speaking in front of a group, to express themselves and so be heard. The chair can create these opportunities at any time by inviting people to gather in small groups where they are seated for a short conversation around more complex matters, for example. Or a more structured small-group process can be put in place for substantial, complex, or contentious matters.

Making sure that the usual suspects don't dominate the microphones is an important strategy. Some churches use indicator cards to allow every member of the meeting to express support or otherwise for the point that a speaker has made, thus making it possible for their perspective to be heard throughout the conversation. Indicator cards also make it easier for some people to indicate whether they wish to speak in favor of a developing idea or to express a reservation.

Giving minority voices an opportunity to speak rather than rushing to close off the discussion once it is obvious that there is a clear majority is an important way to show respect for all the members of the group.

4. Providing Good Information

The introduction of business should be clear and include a presentation of the rationale/reasons for the proposed action. It should provide all the facts and information necessary for people to make a well-informed decision. Time should be taken to understand the implications of the proposed course of action. The implications include not only what will happen if the resolution is passed in its current form but also what is at stake for the people who need to make the decision.

For example, the business before the meeting may be to replace the carpet in the sanctuary. At one level this looks like a straightforward decision: Is the carpet worn out, and do we have the money to replace it? However, by taking time in the introduction phase to unpack what is at stake in making such a decision, it is possible to identify a whole range of issues that may not be apparent in a motion "that the church property committee be authorized to replace the carpet in the Sanctuary."

What might come up if more time is spent in the introduction phase so that transparency and trust are encouraged? Examples of things that might get out in the open at an early stage rather than bubble up during a debate include the following:

- Priorities for use of the church's resources. What else could the money be spent on if this was not done or if it was done more economically?

- Social justice considerations. Where is the carpet made and how; is there a less ecologically damaging option?

- Mission priorities. Does an investment in new sanctuary carpet lock the congregation into this way of worshipping when it may be time to remodel the sanctuary?

- Pastoral issues. Did someone provide funds for the current carpet, and does this affect the way this decision is communicated and implemented?

What are other things?

When these issues are left under the surface, they will affect what people say and how they will want the decision to unfold. These issues may bubble up, but it is far more helpful if they can be encouraged to be identified in the introduction phase. If the choice is only whether or not to change the carpet, the discussion is stunted, and all possible options cannot be canvassed. By being transparent about what is at stake—including for the decision makers—more options can be raised and more appropriate decisions can be made.

5. Safe Spaces

Respect and community are supported by the creation of safe spaces. This means that meeting procedures need to be aware of and address power imbalances. Power imbalances can be based on gender, race, ethnicity, language, ordination, institutional power, capacity to manage well in the prevailing business procedures, and many other factors.

Every member has a personal responsibility to show respect and to try to empower the other members of the community to make their contribution. However, structures and disciplines need to be in place so that best practice is seen as normative and is supported. There are a number of strategies that can assist in making meetings safe places:

- Sensitize people to power imbalances.

- Provide training in how to behave in cross-culturally and gender-sensitive ways.

- Set standards that preclude abusive and denigrating behavior and enforce them through the leadership group; including by the use of liturgical approaches such as prayers of confession.

- Covenant together to act in a healthy and respectful way.

- Use small groups for discussions.

- Allow breaks for groups that feel pressured so that they can go aside for a time and regroup.

6. Submission to the Wisdom of the Group

Many times it will reach a point in a meeting when nearly everyone agrees on the course of action that should be taken; but still people want to continue to make their case. This is an important juncture on the road to discernment and there are two possible routes to take.

One of the primary orientations of a consensus-building approach is to be sure that every person who wants to have an opportunity to contribute is able to do so. It is important not to force the minority voice to buckle over and accept the will of the majority. So the first step to take in this situation is to check whether this person who is unwilling to agree with the proposal has anything to offer that has not already been considered by the group. It may be that this person does and a new fruitful line of conversation may unfold.

However, it is possible to reach the point where there is nothing more to be said. At this point the persons in the minority can hopefully live out of the theological heart of this approach, which is that it is the community in which discernment happens. At such a point it is appropriate for the minority to respect the meeting and with good grace to stand aside. In the Uniting Church in Australia, it is possible for people in this situation to affirm that they have been heard and that they are willing to stand aside in order that the meeting may move to a decision.

7. Seek to Build Consensus

If the goal of church meetings is to allow a group of people to discern the will of God, then it should be expected that more times than not the group will reach consensus on the decisions that should be taken. A vote that seeks to settle a matter by a count of 50 percent + 1 is not keeping faith with the theological commitments that have been affirmed in this book. So if taking a vote at the earliest opportunity to establish a majority position is not keeping faith with the high view of a church meeting, then other steps are required to support the discernment process.

While some matters may come to a point of unanimity or high levels of agreement quite quickly, there are often matters that do not. In these situations, processes are required that help the group identify and document the developing consensus.

Consensus-building is often a very fluid process in which ideas are shared without tying down the discussion with premature documentation of motions and amendments. Moving too early in getting amendments to a motion in front of the meeting forecloses the discussion by narrowing the focus too early. A consensus-building approach has to allow all the issues, experiences, ideas, stories, and theological and other considerations out into the room before "going to print." It needs to allow this even if the way in which the issue got before the meeting was through a formal written petition. The introduction phase is one of the ways in which the subject gets opened up.

As the discussion develops, there are usually themes, considerations, and suggestions that are seen to have significant support. In addition, it will become clear where the use of different words will make it possible for more people to get on board with the developing direction. Meetings need a process that makes it possible for them to gather up this developing consensus into words that can be tested with the group.

Options include a member of the meeting offering to the group what she or he has heard in a form of words that has the necessary precision to allow it to be tested. Another strategy is for two or more active participants in the discussion, including people who have different points of view, to be asked to draft something that they think reflects where there is agreement so far. They can also offer ways to address continuing differences and bring it back to a later session. Where the meeting uses a formal small-group process, the role of the facilitation group is to capture the mind of the meeting by taking the reports from the small groups and offering back what they have heard. This will be done by bringing a report and recommendations for a way forward that is most likely to be supported by the members of the meeting.

Before it is possible for anyone to try and draft words that capture the developing consensus, there need to be ways in which the views of the whole group are identified and not just the views of those who speak at the microphones. There are a number of ways in which this can be easily achieved.

If it is a large meeting with a formal small-group process, the report from the facilitation group is a very straightforward means of hearing what is being said across the membership.

When the conversation is freer flowing, other strategies are required. One that is quite familiar is for the chair of the meeting to summarize what she or he has been hearing and to check that back with the group. In that situation it is not a formal vote to determine the matter, but it is taking a sounding. This process allows that if there is more conversation required, it can be done, but with more focus on the as-yet-unresolved matters. Any member of the meeting can offer this leadership, and the chair can take a similar straw vote, until greater clarity is reached and the group is ready to make the decision.

The World Council of Churches and the World Communion of Reformed Churches have taken up the practice that was developed in the Uniting Church in Australia of using colored indicator cards. These cards allow every member of the meeting to express their mind on a person's speech by showing an orange card if they are warm to what has been said, or by using a blue card if they are cool to the point or still have unresolved concerns with the direction of the discussion. This practice of continuously indicating where people are in the moment helps the group to see where it needs to spend more time, and it also makes possible full participation by even the most reserved person in the room.

Through these and other techniques it is possible to grasp the thoughts of the group—regardless of its size. Consensus is built by knowing where more conversation is required and who has something to contribute, by documenting the direction that has been discerned, and by confirming it with a determination.

CONCLUSION

There is a saying that form follows function. That is to say that if we know the use that we have for something, then we will get the shape of it right. This saying is very applicable to the way in which church meetings are run.

The view that you hold on the nature and purpose of church business meetings will profoundly affect the way you organize your meetings. When people come to these tasks with very different views on what is going on, then they will behave very differently to one another, and conflict, frustration, and confusion are very likely outcomes.

Reflection on the purpose of church meetings is a significant theological endeavor. The answers one reaches will affect what attitudes and behaviors are expected of participants and what practices and processes will be put in place for meetings.

A consensus-building discernment process is a long and well-regarded model among Christian churches. However the practices of many churches do not support this objective; with the result that churches find themselves in ongoing conflict and highly politicized and abusive processes.

It is time to reclaim the tradition of church meetings as community-based consensus-building opportunities. In reclaiming that ground, there is the opportunity to refurbish our practices and recalibrate our attitudes so that we build genuine community and find a more healthy and effective way to make decisions than seems to be the case in many churches today.

REFLECTION QUESTIONS

1. Recall some behaviors you have observed in church meetings. What were the values that were being expressed?

2. What did you learn in this chapter that will make a significant difference in your meetings?

3. What do you think should be the core attitudes and values present in church meetings? How does this compare with the list on pages 50–58.

CHAPTER 4

WHAT KIND OF COMMUNITY ARE WE?

Wesley Congregation prides itself on being a friendly church. In fact, it says so prominently in its weekly newsletter and on its church sign in big bold letters: "Everyone Welcome!"

Wesley was looking for a new pastor. The main candidate, John, made arrangements to visit the congregation for Sunday morning worship and to have a conversation with the key leaders afterward.

Not surprisingly the prospective new pastor was greeted warmly at the church, and everyone wanted to have a chat with him following the service. The subsequent meeting with the local leaders had gone quite well, and toward the end John said, "I have visited this congregation before, you know." The longtime members of the congregation who were serving on the committee were sure that they had never seen him before and wondered when it might have been. John replied: "Oh, I was here at worship three weeks ago, and no one spoke to me."

I suspect that you know of situations like this from your own experience. Many congregations consider themselves friendly, but first-time visitors do not always have a friendly experience. What happens is that members of the congregation do not welcome everyone consistently. Local congregations may view themselves as friendly but don't practice and reflect that self-understanding, and their words and actions do not always match. Sadly, we are well acquainted with the fact that Christians can know the right words to say but don't always live them out. Can you think of some classic disconnects between what congregations say about themselves and how they actually behave?

Let me ask you another question. Do people believe what we write and say about ourselves, or are we judged by what we actually do in real life? I don't think anyone believes what we say if our behavior is not consistent with what we say. The old saying that actions speak louder than words is true.

WHY IS THERE A MISMATCH BETWEEN WHAT CHRISTIANS SAY AND WHAT THEY DO?

Of course, congregations that say things in their newsletter and then fail to deliver are easy marks for criticism. However, many times their failure to have coherence between what they say about themselves and how they actually behave is not because they are committed to a life of hypocrisy. Often this failure to live out the character of the gospel is because many church members are not considering whether their behavior matches what Christians say about themselves. They just don't think about it! The faithful church members at Wesley didn't go to church on Sunday morning with the aim to be unwelcoming; they just didn't think about how a friendly church should behave. Most of the "Wesley" congregations that we know, and cringe at, behave as they do because they do not regularly and actively reflect on whether their behavior is consistent with what is expected of Christians.

Generosity, friendship, and providing the experience of grace are well-known foundations for people coming to faith. The activities that Christians do, which exhibit some of the core characteristics of God, lay the foundation for people to believe the gospel when they hear it. When people experience the character of God in the Christians they encounter, they are more likely to believe their words that speak of God's love and hopes for humanity. The actions of Christians make the words that they say about God plausible.

In contrast, scandal is probably the greatest impediment to the promotion of the Christian faith. Unfortunately scandals in the church happen and are numerous. Every one of them makes it harder for people to believe the good news when they hear it. Whether the scandal is the scourge of child sexual abuse, financial scandals, Christians supporting repressive governments for the church's advantage, a televangelist's inappropriate behavior, or something as local as Christians engaging in unseemly behavior toward one another, the result is the same: People reject the words that the church speaks. Worse, they turn their backs on God.

One of the ongoing activities of many churches that repel members and nonmembers alike is local church fights. People expect a high standard of behavior from Christians when they interact with other people, and especially among themselves. When Christians call one another all sorts of names, belittle one another, tell half-truths (if not outright lies), misrepresent one another, and generally behave like politicians who want to win at all costs—just to get their way in a church meeting—this is an appalling witness from the Christian community. This is the stuff of headlines and heartbreak. It is no wonder that many churches find it difficult to get people to attend meetings and to serve on their judicatories.

THERE IS A SICKNESS IN THE CHURCH

There seems to be a sickness in many parts of church life. For example, there is blindness in many Christians. They do not see how their behavior is disconnected from what the church says about itself. Arguably one of the most widespread and consistent places where this blindness exhibits itself is in meetings of the church. Many churches conduct business in a way that encourages speakers to attack people who hold a different point of view; they honor and reward people who pull down their opponents and create winners and losers. It seems to be more about scoring points than working out what is best for the church. The way we have seen some people behave in a church meeting would have them thrown out of a secular debating society for their unethical, abusive, and disrespectful behavior.

Why does this kind of behavior happen? We don't think that Christians are playing a game of Dr. Jekyll and Mr. Hyde.[1] When people go to church meetings they don't check their Christian principles at the door and plan to be hypocrites. Rather many churches have gotten into bad habits that reflect the dominant culture, and so they use business processes that bring out the worst in us. There is a lack of thoughtful reflection on how our behavior does or does not reflect the things that we believe about ourselves. As noted

---

1. These were characters in a thriller set in Victorian-era England. Dr. Jekyll was a well-regarded and respectable doctor loved by all. At night he uncontrollably changed character and ventured into Hyde Park as a monstrous figure.

previously, this lack of coherence between what to expect of Christians and what we actually do is noticed. It is not a good advertisement of Christianity!

We can no longer assume that people know the appropriate way to behave. Many people, it seems, do not know what is acceptable behavior. The time has come to be clear about how Christians should relate to one another and to make these expectations clear. The expectations must be shaped by the values of the Bible and not the practices of the dominant culture.

There are many Bible passages that speak about how Christians should behave. Our encouragement to you is that you and your local church (or judicatory or conference) take an opportunity to reflect on the appropriateness of your meeting practices in the light of the passages that are most significant for you, for example, 1 Corinthians 13:4-6: "Love is patient, love is kind, it isn't jealous, it doesn't brag, it isn't arrogant, it isn't rude, it doesn't seek its own advantage, it isn't irritable, it doesn't keep a record of complaints, it isn't happy with injustice, but it is happy with the truth."

What would you expect of people in a meeting if they were showing patience and kindness and were not being envious, boastful, or proud? How would people honor one another and avoid being self-seeking while rejoicing in the truth and not holding on to anger? What if your leaders were more trusting, hopeful, and persevering?

Are there ways in which you presently make decisions that work against the expression of these Christian virtues? Our conviction is that there are processes that you can intentionally develop and use that will allow your church's discernment process to better match your words, more than is possible using an outdated parliamentary style of business meeting rules. Tweaking those rules and how they are used is not good enough. A consensus-building style of decision-making will bring coherence between what the Bible expects of Christians and what you do in your church meetings.

Many people know that what they see happening in church meetings is offensive to the gospel. Across the world, people from all backgrounds are crying out for another way of talking together and making decisions. People have had enough of the way the church does business. As someone reading this book, you are probably one of those people who knows that something is wrong. You have probably thought a lot about how to make church meetings more inclusive of everyone, how to make them more respectful of participants, and how to make them collaborative as decisions are sought and made. You are not alone in that insight and hope.

With so many people yearning for a more Christian way of discerning what God wants for their church community, we might wonder why things have not changed. For most people, the reason is that they don't see any alternative to the traditional parliamentary process or *Robert's Rules of Order*. So they tinker at the edges and hope that a few modest changes will overcome the cut and thrust "winner-takes-all" culture of this inherently combative process. However, it will never be enough. The culture of the parliamentary style of decision-making is theologically, sociologically, and culturally antithetical to the way the Bible teaches us to relate to one another, to how wisdom is discerned today, and to how people make decisions in other areas of their life.

Having tried to make the best of the current parliamentary format in church meetings, many people give up hope because there seems to be a lack of alternatives. The good news is that there are options. These options are built around a commitment to a consensus-building approach for decision-making. They are collaborative, open, engaging, and respectful processes that empower the participation of all and make spaces where the Holy Spirit can lead Christians to discernment. These processes are not new. The Quaker tradition has always followed processes that seek a common mind among the gathered community—what they call "the mind of the meeting"—before they are prepared to say that they have discerned the will of God for their community of faith. Many small congregations will only make decisions after there has been plenty of time to explore all the issues involved and to get everyone on board; because they know that you can't move a small congregation forward on an issue when a significant minority is opposed to a decision. In 1994, the Uniting Church in Australia adopted a consensus process as its Standing Orders for the meetings of its National Council—the Assembly. Since 2000, the Manual for Meetings has been the Standing Orders for all meetings of the Uniting Church in Australia.

Faithful discernment requires that the same level of value be given to ensuring that the way decisions are made reflects the values of the Christian community as is given to what the decisions are.

Reflection on the kind of community that we are leads us to make certain commitments to one another about how we will behave. Putting behaviors and practices in place that support those commitments allows us to affirm that being is just as important as doing when it comes to bearing witness to Christ.

THE FOUNDATIONS FOR A HEALTHIER DISCERNMENT PROCESS

If you are interested in encouraging a new, healthier, and more effective way to discern the will of God for your congregation, judicatory, or denomination, then there a few simple steps that you can take to get started. In chapters 5 and 8 we will share with you in much more detail what is involved in constructing a consensus-building approach to discernment, but you can start thinking into this space right now.

First, consider what kind of church you are. What does your local church or denomination say are its values? When you reflect on your values, it is possible to consider what commitments such values require you to make to the other members of your community of faith. Values lead to commitments that must then be supported by practices. For example, if I value a healthy body then I will make a number of commitments to myself around diet, lifestyle, and exercise. However, those commitments will mean nothing if I do not then identify behaviors and practices that support them. In this example the practices I adopt will include exercise plans, shopping lists, planning to get enough sleep, perhaps where I live, etc. It is the practices that we put in place that support the values that we say we hold.

When we think about the way church meetings operate, the same principles apply: Values should lead to commitments, which then lead to practices/behaviors. When we get these three things—values, commitments, and practices—calibrated, then our church meetings will consistently demonstrate that we mean what we say.

We invite you to ask yourself what kind of church you are. What do you say about yourself as a local congregation or as a denomination? What are the key values that you are known for or which you promote about yourself? There is no right or wrong answer here. Different Christian groups have different emphases and that is OK. The important thing is that what people see of us—in all our activities—is consistent with what we say about ourselves.

If coherence between what we say about ourselves and our actions is important to external observers, it is significant to members of the church too. If people are going to change the way they behave—including in church business meetings—then they need to see how the new way of doing things is consistent with their values. If they cannot see this link, then the changes are open to being seen as a fad or an imposition that it not owned or meaningful to the people who have to put the changes into effect. However, when time is taken to help people see how a change in the way things are done is being true to themselves, then you will find commitment and consistency in making the changes. The changes will feel good because people can say, "This is who we are!"

A CASE STUDY FROM THE WORLD COMMUNION OF REFORMED CHURCHES (WCRC)

The WCRC is an international ecumenical organization for churches that come from the Reformed, Congregational, and Waldensian traditions. Examples of other world confessional bodies include the World Methodist Council and the World Lutheran Federation.

In 2004, when the World Alliance of Reformed Churches (one of the predecessor bodies to the WCRC) met in Accra, Ghana, it made its first use of some tools that had been drawn from the consensus practices of the Uniting Church in Australia. Prior to its 2010 inaugural meeting as the WCRC at Grand Rapids, Michigan, the new body resolved to build on this experience and adopted additional rules for use in part of its meeting that would further express a consensus-building model.

As it prepared for its General Council meeting in Leipzig, Germany, in 2017, the planning group discussed what kind of business procedures it would use. The executive and its planning committee decided to build on the procedures that were implemented in 2010. The planning group reflected on the principles that should shape its business procedures. It was not just enough to follow a trend. Rather the processes adopted for the meeting had to make sense to the members and align with the character of the organization.

The World Communion of Reformed Churches describes itself as a communion that is committed to justice. Therefore the WCRC needed procedures that would help it to be a communion that lived justly. This was being true to its character and goals. As a result of focusing on their core values, they were able to affirm a number of commitments that they needed to make to one another.

The values are communion and justice. The commitments that arise from these values have been identified as respect, patience, trust, shared goals, vulnerability, empowerment for all, values-based discussions and decisions, and decisions that are owned by the most people possible. After reflecting on the commitments that members needed to make to one another in the light of what the WCRC says are its values, a number of practices and behaviors could be named.

A. IN SUPPORT OF THE VALUE "COMMUNION"

Commitment: Be Respectful
Practices and Behaviors

- Create spaces where as many people as possible can make contributions.

- Enhance the capacity of people to contribute, not just through interpretation but also through cultural sensitivity and dismantling and addressing power imbalances.

- Accept that people make contributions in a variety of ways, not just through academic, linear, rational arguments.

- Take the time to listen and attend carefully and fully to one another.

- Provide members with the opportunity to receive and welcome views even when they are at odds with what they currently think.

Commitment: Be Patient
Practices and Behaviors

- Take the time needed so that each person can think about the issues and find their voice into the process.

- Recognize that relationships are equally—possibly more—important than the task itself. So take the time for stories and understanding one another.

Commitment: Trust One Another
Practices and Behaviors

- Expect that people really are on the same side.

- Engage in activities that enhance trust.

- Where trust is absent, take that seriously and address the experiences that have led to such a situation.

Commitment: Shared Goals
Practices and Behaviors

- Use processes that enable collaboration.

- Develop shared understanding of the issues and possible solutions.

- Seek consensus so far as possible.

Commitment: Being Vulnerable
Practices and Behaviors

- Allow opportunities for people to share what is really important to them—emotionally, spiritually, theologically, relationally, practically, and so on.

- Expect that people are prepared to be changed by their encounters with others.

B. IN SUPPORT OF THE VALUE "JUSTICE"

Commitment: Empowerment of All
Practices and Behaviors

- Deliver good information in a timely manner in a way that means that all people know what they are talking about and what is at stake.

- Take power imbalances seriously and work constructively to help the powerless to find their voice.

Commitment: Values-Based Discussions and Decisions
Practices and Behaviors

- Encourage speakers who are presenting proposals to name the goals, visions, and values they are affirming and not just the actions and outcomes that they are seeking.

- Do not allow the claimed views of people who are not in the meeting to hold sway.

Commitment: Generate Support for Decisions
Practices and Behaviors

- Just decisions do not reflect the wishes of the privileged elite.

- Processes should make it possible for decisions to be owned by as many people as possible.

- Setting up for a simple majority for a decision sells such a goal short.

Having taken the time to name and affirm its values, the WCRC was in a position to state clearly what commitments the members needed to make to one another. After the values and commitments were named, then practices could be put in place to support and express those values and commitments.

The practices in the case study are written in quite general terms. The necessary step before the General Council meeting in 2017 was to write rules for the business meeting that reflect the practices that have been affirmed. No worries!

WHO ARE YOU AND WHAT ARE YOU GOING TO DO ABOUT IT?

You can change the way that people behave in church meetings for the better. The change has to be values driven. So the place to start is thinking about the values that are owned or could be named by your church.

Some of the ways churches describe themselves include Bible believing, friendly, Christ centered, inclusive, mission focused, and so on. If these values are important in your church, then these are some of the things that you might think about as you explore the commitments that you want to make to one another.

This list of things you might want to think about, or the questions that you might want to ask in your community, is not meant to be exhaustive but rather a sample of possible lines for conversation. Conversations around your values should allow you to articulate the commitments that you will make to one another as you engage in a process of discernment within your church community.

In the following section we will not try to say what your commitments should be, much less try to drill down to the practices that support the commitments you want to make. These steps will be looked at more closely in chapter 8. Nevertheless feel free to think about it if you are ready to do so. Remember, we are thinking here about how you might change the way you undertake the journey of discernment so that it is consistent with your values. It is not hard to see how this framework can also be used to reflect on your church's practices in a number of different areas.

Consider the values that your church claims for itself. Ask the question: "If this is what we value, then how does that affect how we behave in meetings?" To answer this question, you need to unpack the implications that arise from these values. Following are some common church values. If these are your church values, you can use these questions to get you started. If your church has other values, then use these examples as illustrations of the type of discussion that you will have.

Bible believing: Which parts of the Bible should be taken into account when thinking about discernment as a Christian community? How is the Bible to be heard? Who may speak, and what "credentials" will you require from people? What do you commit to do together so that the community is better placed to be led by the Holy Spirit?

Friendly: What do friendly Christians do for one another? How do they deal with conflict? Who gets to be in the group? What practices sustain friendship?

Christ-centered: What would Jesus do if he were leading your meeting? What practices help a community to remain Christ centered? If the church is the body of Christ, then how is the whole body included in the discernment process?

Inclusive: Who is included, and how do they know it? How does an inclusive community deal with different passionately held views? How does an inclusive community take care of people who are not in the majority?

Mission focused: What behaviors would allow people to look at your church meeting and say, "Look at those Christians. See how they love one another!"? If the unity of Christians is the key to the world believing (John 17), how is unity encouraged and supported? Who gets to decide what the mission will be, and how is that decision made? How do you relate to the members of this community so that they can be part of the mission?

Our behavior as Christians in a discernment process is as important as the decisions that we make. The process that we follow should be a reflection of our values, and the commitments that we make to one another should arise from those values. The way we conduct a discernment process—the practices and processes that we put in place—should be designed to support these commitments.

The parliamentary style of decision-making is at odds with the values and commitments that many Christians hold. The church needs a corporate discernment process that is more aligned to what being a faithful church looks like when it is located in a western liberal democracy in the twenty-first century. The corporate discernment process that best achieves this alignment, and greatly enhances the prospect of being faithful, is a consensus-building process.

REFLECTION QUESTIONS

1. Can you think of any places in your context where there is not alignment between what your organization says about itself and how it behaves?

2. What does your organization say are its core values and identity? How are these reflected in the way that you make decisions?

3. How would you go about having a conversation about aligning values and business meeting practices in your organization?

ACTIVITY: DECISION-MAKING: PAST, PRESENT, AND FUTURE

Get together with a group of leaders in your ministry setting and complete this diagram. This group may be the leaders in your church council or the planning group in your congregation, a district or conference board staff member. Have enough copies of the ACA Diagram to distribute to each person.

Say: "Think carefully about your experience, knowledge, and feelings about making decisions in your congregation (or ministry setting). If you were to be a part of an effort to create an effective decision-making process:

COMPLETE THE FIRST COLUMN

(Do this section of the chart individually in quiet.)

Say: "Let's look at the first column—ACHIEVE. What things would you want us to achieve or accomplish in the next year so we make good decisions together?" Provide a few examples: "Let people know in advance when major decisions need to be made, provide training in the new process to be used, send leaders copies of any material relevant to the decision so they can read it in advance of the meeting, allow enough time, etc."

Allow 10 minutes for people to complete their responses.

Call time and ask the participants to share their responses. Note: If some participants contribute responses that you do not understand, carefully ask them to explain why their responses matter to them. Use probing questions to help them clarify their responses. ("I don't know what this means 'All always.' Is it meant to be 'Always ask'?") Ask the group after each response shared: "Can we support that response? Are we willing to do it?" If there is not support for a comment, ask the group, "Can we word the response in a way that would be acceptable to you?" Invite participants to write responses in the first column of their ACA Diagram Worksheet.

Write the responses on newsprint.

Ask the group if there are any other things they need to accomplish together in order to be in a position to make good decisions. Add additional remarks.

73

COMPLETE THE SECOND COLUMN

(Do this section of the diagram in pairs.)

Say: "Let's look at the second column—CONTINUE. In our current method of making decisions, what would you want us to preserve or continue?" Provide some examples to the group: "Involve everyone in the process, be respectful to one another, listen deeply, allow people time to voice their views, surround the session with prayer, and so on."

Allow ten minutes for people to work in pairs and add their responses to the second column.

Call time and invite people to share their responses. Invite participants to add group responses to the middle column of their ACA Diagram Worksheet.

Write all responses on newsprint.

Ask the group if there are any other things they want to preserve of the current method of making decisions. Add those responses.

COMPLETE THE LAST COLUMN

(Do this section as a group.)

Say: "Let's complete the last column—AVOID—as a group. When you think of a good process to discern God's will as we make decisions together, what specific cautions might you suggest in order to avoid conflicts and failure?" Provide some examples for the group: "Get into interpersonal arguments, foster a win-lose mentality, ignore the quiet voices in the group, or not include people who will be impacted by the decision."

Allow enough time for everyone to contribute a response. Invite participants to add responses to their ACA Diagram under the last column.

Write the response on newsprint. Be sure to clarify responses that you do not understand.

Ask the group if there are any additional things to consider as they avoid blocks to making good decisions together.

Important for the group leader: Have a completed ACA Diagram prepared for people using the notes on the newsprint of the conversation. Review the sheet at your next meeting and ask for any revisions. Ask leaders to keep a copy of this sheet with them at meetings so that their comments and actions align with the ACA's intent when making decisions together.

MAKING GOOD DECISIONS: ACA CHART

Purpose: Surface our shared values related to making good decisions together as a Christian community. We will use this sheet to guide our words and actions when making decisions in the future.

When making decisions, I believe...

ACHIEVE (things we must accomplish in order to be a faithful church)	CONTINUE (things we value and wish to continue to be a faithful church)	AVOID (things that must not occur or happen if we are to be a faithful church)

Review your ACA Diagram. What have you learned about making good decisions together in community? What is important to you? What are you willing to do?

A STEP–BY–STEP PROCESS TO SUCCESSFULLY ENGAGE CHURCH GROUPS IN CONTEMPORARY DISCERNMENT

We can only be wise together.

—Kathryn Hannah Schriver (my grandmother)

When we dream alone it is only a dream, but when many dream together it is the beginning of a new reality.

—Friedensreich Hundertwasser

INTRODUCTION: ARE WE THERE YET?

Mount Erebus is the southernmost active volcano on earth. Air New Zealand operated a sightseeing excursion from Auckland to Antarctica featuring an extraordinary view of the mountain and surrounding area. On November 28, 1979, Flight 901 took off with 257 passengers and crew onboard and ended in absolute disaster. What happened? Tragically, navigational error! The flight path coordinates were changed the evening before the flight departed, but the crew were not notified of the change. Therefore, as they descended in whiteout conditions, they thought they were a safe distance from the volcano over McMurdo Sound. Because they could not check their surroundings, they were relying totally on their equipment. Sadly, they were actually twenty-seven miles to the east and directly in the path of the volcano. Lesson: Don't rely entirely on your autopilot; check your context, and anticipate changes.

It's time to take stock of our ways of making decisions and to see if they are really getting us where we need to go as a faith community. Rather than rely on the autopilot of outdated or undermining processes, which repeat the same mistakes over and over, we need to get back on a firm path as a community of faith. When you think of your current process of making decisions, are you satisfied that those decisions align with the values embedded in your organization? Does the way you make decisions form a stronger community and result in good decisions?

How many times have you been in a meeting in which

- poor preparation paralyzes a group

- after an energetic debate, no decision is ever reached

- a new mission project is up for discussion, yet people do not get engaged and the ministry falls flat

- the loudest voice sidetracks or sways the work of the group

- the process you use to make decisions creates divisions with winners and losers

- it takes three months to reach a conclusion and three times that long to implement it

These are serious signs that you need a new process!

There are several distinct phases in making and implementing good decisions. The best decisions are made, and get put into effect, when people enter into an intentional four-phase process of decision-making. Leaders should guide their group through a comprehensive process that includes preparation, invitation, engaging participation in making the decision, and supporting the successful implementation of the decision. To do anything less often creates conflict, confusion, and competition.

Naturally, some items of routine business or matters that are returning for further consideration may not require a detailed application of all the phases in the cycle. Nevertheless, it is always worth checking that people have been prepared and invited into the process and that strategies are in place to make the experience a positive one. For substantial business, it will be helpful to concentrate on the four-part process and to use more of the resources that have been provided in support of implementing it. The material can be tailored to the reader's unique setting and circumstances. It is adaptable to different size groups on local, national, and global gatherings and issues of various levels of complexity.

SEEKING GOD'S WILL TOGETHER

There are many decisions an organization needs to make. Some are routine and not particularly complex. In such situations, the need for formality or planning may seem to be more effort than is required. When meeting planners do not reflect on the nature of the business that is before them, and plan accordingly, they often run on an automatic system. This results in the more complex and contentious issues not receiving the careful attention they deserve. This is a mistake.

There are issues that warrant special care and attention. Therefore, we encourage you, as you prepare your agenda and consider the business that will be coming before your group, to ask of every item in your agenda, "Is this something for which we need to prepare people, invite them into the process, use a different process for decision-making, and take special care to ensure that the lines of accountability are clear?"

DEFINING THE TERMS OF ENGAGEMENT

Discernment is a spiritual process of reaching a place where we can say we have discovered the will of God. It is about making decisions that accomplish our God-given purpose in ways that people can understand and support. The more important the issue, the more likely there will be conflict (see chapter 2). Consensus occurs when a whole group comes to the understanding that they have discovered the will of God for their place and time. Moreover, people are able to support it. Key questions include the following:

- What is God calling us to do in this place and time?
- What unique contribution will we make in our community and world?

Romans 12:1-2 reminds us that practicing discernment produces transformation:

> So, brothers and sisters, because of God's mercies, I encourage you to present your bodies as a living sacrifice that is holy and pleasing to God. This is your appropriate priestly service. Don't be conformed to the patterns of this world, but be transformed by the renewing of your minds so that you can figure out what God's will is—what is good and pleasing and mature.

Discernment calls forth a responsibility from the group's participants to

- speak up when they do not understand something; ask questions
- help create an atmosphere of trust and respect
- listen actively to one another
- think before you speak
- embrace disagreement as a way to seek common ground
- state your perspective and let it go
- involve all the right people (especially those affected)
- establish/remind one another of your guiding values and principles
- pray without ceasing
- select an option that seems consistent with what God is doing among you
- patiently wait on the Holy Spirit to reveal a way forward

The following Bible passages offer some important lessons about discernment:

Proverbs 4:7
(What does a wise heart seek?)

Proverbs 18:15
(What do we seek together?)

Isaiah 8:19-20
(What is the role of scripture?)

John 5:30
(Whose will do we seek when making decisions?)

1 Corinthians 13:1-3
(What is the role of love?)

1 Corinthians 12:3
(What is the role of Jesus Christ?)

Philippians 1:9-10
(What is the role of community?)

James 1:5
(Who gives wisdom?)

What do these passages teach you about how to make decisions?

CONSENSUS: BUILDING CHRISTIAN COLLECTIVE INTELLIGENCE

Consensus decision-making is discovering God's will together. It is a way of giving us the confidence that we have discovered God's will on a matter under the guidance of the Holy Spirit. Call it "Christian Collective Intelligence." It is based on the idea that people should have control over their lives together and that power should be shared rather than concentrated in the hands of a few. It is conversation between people who respect one another. Further, consensus is a dynamic way of reaching a decision. For consensus to work, certain conditions must be met:

81

- desiring to seek common goal
- forming an intentional community
- committing to reaching consensus together
- hearing the marginalized and ensuring the decision works for them as well
- having trust and openness
- having sufficient time
- following a clear process
- everyone actively participating
- paraphrasing or summarizing what you hear other people saying
- respecting diversity and dissent
- desiring to continually improve the decision-making system
- having good facilitation

A common complaint about moving to consensus is: "But it takes too long!" Try these methods to effectively use your time:

- Distribute information in advance of the meeting for people to review.
- Delegate details to working groups rather than doing it in the total group.
- Form a facilitation team to synthesize the group's ideas into a proposal.
- Use a trained facilitator.
- Keep accurate meeting notes to avoid revisiting decisions.

RECONSIDERING ROBERT'S RULES OF ORDER

Rather than follow a spiritual approach, most churches today use another method to make decisions called *Robert's Rules of Order* that was modeled after the way decisions are made in governmental meetings. After the Civil War, Henry Martyn Robert was chairing the trustee meeting of New Bedford

Baptist Church in Massachusetts. He had a miserable experience; the men in the room could not agree on anything or make any decisions. Robert felt frustrated with this waste of time and vowed never to chair another meeting without clear rules and procedures in place. As a former a US Army officer he turned to parliamentary procedures to base his work. That's how we got *Robert's Rules of Order*, which is now in its eleventh edition.

Maybe it's time to break the rules. Let's be clear: These rules can make a meeting more efficient, provide structure, and ensure that participants have equal rights and responsibilities. On the downside, these rules can create problems:

- It is not a spiritual practice, but we are a community of faith.

- The rules are an intricate series of motions that can be confusing.

- The will of the majority prevails.

- The rules create power imbalances.

- By focusing on "one person, one vote," it elevates the individual's view and vote, not a community's perspective.

- It creates divisions with winners and losers.

- The process works well for those who know the rules best and can use them for those own purpose.

- Discussion can be cut short when someone "Calls for the Question," which can force the vote.

COMPARISON OF ROBERT'S RULES OF ORDER AND A CONSENSUS-BUILDING APPROACH

There are fundamental differences in the way decisions are reached using consensus-building and using *Robert's Rules of Order*. See the chart below for these differences.

ITEM	CONSENSUS	ROBERT'S RULES OF ORDER
Orientation	Community	Individual
Leader	Facilitator	Presiding Officer
Participants	Everyone	Voting members
Goal	Transformational	Transactional
Process	Engage in dialogue and share information to reach conclusion	Follow the rules to reach a vote
Agreement	Reached by negotiation, developing new ideas, and willingness to meet the needs of others	Reached by majority rule
Focus	What does God expect of us?	What do we want to do next?
Support	All vested and empowered	Those in the majority are the biggest advocates
Communication	Interpersonal Respectful conversation and exchange of ideas	Independent Debate Guided by Process
Environment	Safe for all to participate in a healthy discourse	Personal Guided by process
Perspective	Theocratic	Democratic
Most helpful	• When everyone's input is desired • When there are culturally and socially diverse groups of people in the meeting • To deal with significant matters that affect the entire group • Various options are present • Time can be spent to explore options • Differences between people are seen as gifts and stimulants to greater wisdom • Discerning God's will together is as important as making the decision together • Synthesis of ideas makes the strongest decision • About unity, not uniformity • Maximize support before reaching a decision	• When a quick decision is needed • To deal with routine business • An issue has almost full consensus • When clear alternatives have been identified • People are comfortable with the rules • When delaying a decision is not an option • Representatives of the group are empowered to decide • A group gets stuck

Least helpful	• Emergency situations that need immediate action • People fall into groupthink • Issue is a simple yes or no • There is a lack of trust in a group • When there are obstinate people who will not stop presenting the same position over and over	• When participants agree to a position they do not support • When the support of the minority is needed in the implementation of the decision • For generating creative options leading to a stronger decision

A BASIC PLATFORM

The following diagram shows a basic cycle that enhances the whole decision-making process, maximizing people's capacity to participate, to understand what is happening, and to have the decisions implemented.

STEP 1: PREPARE	STEP 3: DECIDE
STEP 2: INVITE	STEP 4: IMPLEMENT

The following are the four steps in the cycle of discernment:

Step 1: Preparation—Name the issue(s), think about meeting preparation including who will fill key roles, seek prayer support, and set meeting guidelines.

Step 2: Invitation—Let people know what the issues will be and invite their prayers and presence. Prime the process so people are not hitting the issue cold.

Step 3: Decision Point—Decide which items of business will best be addressed through the various tools that are used as part of a consensus-building approach to discernment and plan the meeting accordingly.

Step 4: Implementation—Decide who will take responsibility for the implementation of the decision, establish timelines for action, and evaluate the process. Celebrate concluding the process.

Organizations make simple and complex decisions. They make choices that affect very few people and others that have a significant impact on the organization and its members. The recommendations provided in the four steps of the discernment cycle, which are quite comprehensive, are particularly relevant for major issues. You will need to take into account the size of your organization and the complexity of the issue that is being addressed before making a judgment on whether it is helpful to use all of the options that are presented. Even though this is the case, the four-phase movement of the cycle, and the thoughtful preparation that it affirms, should be applied as appropriate to the normal agenda of an organization.

STEP 1: PREPARATION

Get organized for a healthy and effective discernment process. A discernment process will be effective when both the decision-makers and those who are affected by those decisions are well informed about the topic that will be addressed, are encouraged to prepare for the meeting, are adequately supported and resourced for their role, and are given ways to engage with the process.

There are four components to effectively preparing a group for making decisions: designing the process, identifying the implementation team and its task, involving the people who are affected by any decision, and resourcing the decision-makers.

A. Designing the Process

1. The Agenda

Every meeting has an agenda. Responsibility for developing the agenda is given to persons who fill certain roles, depending on the organization. For example, it is usually the chairperson and secretary; or in congregations, it may include the pastor if she or he is not the chairperson. Larger organizations may have an executive or a business committee that fulfills this role. Agendas should never be produced with input from only one person.

An agenda is an order of business that takes into account the priorities of an organization and the way it manages its time. In organizations that do not routinely use a consensus approach in their meetings, or the four-step cycle of discernment, it is necessary to identify which item(s) of business is of such importance that the four-step cycle is very deliberately used. The group that is responsible for developing the agenda should formally identify the business that will be brought into this process. In addition it should name and document which elements of a consensus-building approach and the four-step cycle of discernment are appropriate for this business.

2. Managing the Business

All organizations have customs as well as formal rules that guide the way that they do business. Most organizations operate on autopilot when it comes to process, even if the flight path is leading to disaster. Don't do this!

Agendas should reflect thoughtful conclusions about how much time a piece of business will take, how the business is best brought before the meeting, and when is the best time to address particular business. When a special meeting of a congregation is required, or if there is a particularly contentious item of business on an agenda, particular care should be taken to decide when and where a meeting will be held and who needs to be present.

A task that the group should address at this early stage is the development of clear understanding of what is hoped to be accomplished through this piece of business. What is the outcome that is sought? For example: Is the desired outcome to set future directions for the organization; to make decisions about staffing; to address a conflict in the organization? Set realistic goals and expectations for the session(s). It is also important to consider the lead time that is needed before the business arrives on the agenda, so that when it is before the meeting for decision, it will be well handled.

3. Planning the Next Steps

Once the group that has responsibility to develop the agenda has decided that a particular piece of business warrants careful implementation of the four-phase cycle of discernment, then a group to design and implement the process should be set up. This process planning group will comprise five to seven key leaders who have the role of designing and guiding the process. It may include the pastor, meeting chair, a communications person, and some-one who is familiar with the logistics of the location so that rooms can be booked, hospitality organized, and so on. If later it is decided that an external trainer or facilitator is to be part of the process design, then these people can be added to the process planning group. A clear list of responsibilities should be documented for this group, including timelines and lines of accountability.

Having done this preparatory work, the group that develops the agenda should take its proposed course of action to the decision-making body for endorsement. Consensus is best built by including people at every stage. By getting the meeting attendees to agree to a special process, the members are much more likely to support its implementation.

B. The Task of the Process Planning Group

1. Develop a Master Plan for the Process

Before commencing any part of the process, a complete plan should be developed that covers all the elements of the four-step process. It is crucial that all the elements work together in a timely way so that they enhance the effectiveness of the process.

The agenda for the process planning group can be summarized as decid-ing on the best way to process the business, identifying the resources and sup-port that will be required by the decision-makers and the community affected by any potential decision, developing communication plans, and putting in place all the practical arrangements that are essential for an effective discern-ment process.

2. *Identify the Information Required and Plan Its Distribution*

The decision-makers and the community affected by any potential decision must know about the process and how it will work. At several points in the four-step process there are opportunities to ensure that people have the information that they need so that they can participate in the process.

3. *Design the Deliberation Phase (See Chapter 8)*

The deliberation phase is step three in the cycle. It is what happens in the meeting that will make the decision. When this aspect of the design is completed, a number of tasks will flow for the organizers. The detail will depend on which parts of a consensus process are chosen. For example:

- Who will prepare the petition/proposal and the rationale in support of the direction that is being recommended, present it to the meeting, and respond to questions for clarification?
- Will there be a small group process? If so:
  - Who will recruit the members of the facilitation team?
  - Who will assign people to the small groups?
  - Who will ensure recruitment of recorders and leaders for the groups?
  - Will an external facilitator be used to resource the process by doing such tasks as preparing the discussion questions and reporting sheets?
  - What rooms and other work spaces need to be identified and booked?
  - What training is required for the facilitation team, the chair of the meeting, the meeting secretary, and small group leaders?
  - What materials and equipment are needed, and who will ensure that they are in place?
- How much time will be required to roll out the whole process from the establishment of the process planning group and its work (step one); through to engaging people in the process (step two); to the deliberation and decision-making phase

(step three); and finally to communicating, implementing, and celebrating the decision?

- Do key leaders know their responsibilities?

4. Other Considerations

Will funding be necessary to pay for a facilitator, supplies, meeting space, and refreshments? If so, a budget needs to be developed and submitted to the relevant meeting.

Identify the areas of work that will require teams to be put together; then appoint conveners and oversee the recruitment, orientation, and training of the teams.

There will be quite a few tasks that flow from considering the next two areas of step one in the cycle. They are so important that they warrant detailed consideration. After ensuring that those steps have been adequately addressed, it is also helpful to ask, "What else is needed to ensure a healthy, well-supported, and effective process?"

C. Involving the People Who Are Affected

If people are going to support a decision that might be demanding or challenging, then they need to be included in the process from the very beginning in a way that is appropriate. What works for a congregation may be different in parts to a denomination-wide issue. Even so there are many elements that are consistent: such as maintaining good communication strategies, building trust and confidence in the process, and encouraging prayer for the process and leaders. The process planning group will take its context into account and design the process accordingly.

1. Developing Communication Strategies

Let people know what is going on. Every step along the way people should be kept up to date on what is happening and why. The focus for the communication strategy will include telling people about

- the business that has been identified for this careful process

- why it is so important to the organization

- names of members of the process planning group

- the process that has been developed, including the identity of any external facilitator and the date and venue for the decision-making meeting

- the way in which people can be involved in the discernment process

- the final decision and related matters

2. Building Confidence in the Process

When people don't have confidence in a process, the decision-makers, or the leaders of the process, then they are far less likely to support a decision. Indeed, a lack of trust will nearly always lead to strong resistance to a new process and any decision that comes through it.

It is imperative that the leadership of an organization trust the members and provide them with accurate and timely information about every aspect of the business and the process that is being used. Ways to do this include providing information on the key leaders including any external facilitator or resource persons, explaining the significance of the issue before the organization, and dealing with uncertainty, tensions, and fears in the decision-making group and/or the people who will be impacted by any decision.

3. Fostering a Spiritual Connection with the Process

Foster and support a spiritual posture in people as they attend to the process. Call a season of prayer for the process and provide devotional resources. Invite people to respond to the season of prayer in concrete ways.

D. Resourcing the Decision-Makers

As the process planning group undertakes its task, it will identify a number of areas in which training and resources are required. Worship, prayer, and other spiritual disciplines should always be included in this list. The goal is to put the decision-makers in the best possible position to make a good decision.

In contentious matters, or the implementation of a new process, organizations often underestimate the value of engaging external facilitators. However, they are often a high-value resource even if they charge a fee. Their presence frees others to participate more fully, ensures an impartial implementation of the process, brings a non-biased perspective to the situation, and offers relevant experience, resources, and training to support the leadership and the meeting in the fulfillment of their roles.

Create a safe, supportive environment for the process. Establish a behavioral guideline covenant and other documents that make expectations about behavior clear to all.

Larger meetings may make use of observers who monitor the emotional climate of the group by watching body language and who speaks and how often and providing a report at the appropriate time so improvements can be made. Depending on the process selected, additional support may be required; for example, additional note takers and projector operators/administrative support.

STEP 2: INVITE TO DISCERN

If decisions are going to be owned within the community on whose behalf they are made, then that community needs to be drawn into the process as much as possible. Let people know what the issues will be and invite their prayers and presence. For both the decision-makers and the people affected by the decision, it is crucial to prime the process so people are not hitting the issue cold.

Here are some of the ways you can invite people to participate in the process:

1. **Decide who needs to be at the meeting**, for example, church leaders and members, as well as those affected by the decision such as stakeholders and community leaders knowledgeable about the issue.

2. **Develop a clear communication plan**. Options include the following:

   - Send an open letter to the congregation (or religious group) and community that
     - shares the details and purpose of the meeting
     - explains why this process is vital to the church
     - requests prayer for leaders, participants, process, and outcome

- encloses a response card to indicate willingness to participate

- Make numerous announcements (in the worship bulletin, newsletter, e-mail chain, web page, etc.)

- Promote using multimedia (YouTube/Video, Facebook, DVDs, presentations, website, or PowerPoint)

3. **Practice the Means of Grace** (Vital Piety and Acts of Compassion) as a faith community.

4. **Introduce the process leaders to the congregation and explain** why both the decision-making session and their participation are crucial.

STEP 3: DELIBERATION AND DECISION

This step is the heart of the decision-making process.

Something that is often assumed in church meetings is that everyone knows how the decision-making process works. Frequently this is not the case. However, when an alternative process is being employed, there will be a greater number of people who are unfamiliar with the process. Uncertainty creates anxiety, and anxiety gives rise to defensive behaviors. People need to understand the process in order to participate fully. People need to know what is going to happen next!

One of the foundational elements of a discernment process that is built on consensus-building principles is the empowering of everyone to participate as equals. Knowledge is power, and so the first rule in this sort of process is that everyone must have access to the same knowledge. There are many kinds of knowledge that people require if they are going to be empowered to participate in discerning together the will of God for their organization. People need to know what issues are being addressed, the outcomes that will flow from the options that are before them, the needs and concerns of the other members of the group, and how the process works. At this point the focus is on this last point. The normative practice in meetings should be a clear presentation of what is going to happen, who is going to do it, why these steps are necessary, and how they all fit together as part of the journey to discernment.

There are four phases in the deliberative phase of a consensus-building approach, which are then followed by the step of making the decision:

1. Gather the Community: Drawing Close to God and One Another

 a. Welcome

 b. Worship or an appropriate devotion

 c. Build community

 d. Set boundaries/guidelines for participation

 e. Adopt the agenda, break times, and so on

 f. Provide an overview of the consensus process

2. Information Phase: Where the Issue Is Presented

 a. Present the issue/topic to be discussed with relevant information

 b. Share material related to the issue/topic, including the goal/rationale behind the proposed course of action. Encourage presentation of the values and goals that are present in the petition and not just the words

 c. Receive, and respond to, as many questions for clarification as are needed to ensure that people understand the issues that are before them

 d. Allow space for speakers to share what is important for them as they consider the issue

3. Deliberation Phase: Where the Creative Options Surface and Shape the Direction of the Decision

The deliberation phase is when the decision-makers consult together and seek to understand the impact of the proposal on them and others, to share experiences, feelings, and theological and other perspectives as they consider the issue or petition. It is a time to begin identifying whether the petition is acceptable in its current form or whether there are other ways of achieve the goals that have been suggested.

As the discussion unfolds, alternative words and directions for action begin to surface and are tested as replacements for the original petition. Gradually a form of words is identified that has the highest level of support among the group.

There are a wide variety of tools that can be used in the deliberation phase as a way of assisting the expression of the growing discernment and for assessing the level of support for developing ideas. These elements are outlined in detail in chapter 8.

4. Determination Phase: Making the Decision

At some point in the process it is necessary to make a decision. It may be a decision to act in the direction that was originally recommended. Perhaps it is a decision to defer a final decision and to do more work. It could be a decision that no action of the kind anticipated is required at this time. It may be that a totally new sense of the Holy Spirit's leading has arisen and the process of discernment has led to a new insight. There are many kinds of decisions, and a good process will always come to some decision.

Different polities and church rules operate when a decision is to be taken. However, whether the decision is taken by identifying a consensus, by ballots, by show of hands, or by stamping of feet, at some point the meeting will express its mind on the discernment that it has reached. The consensus-building approach advocated for in this book can be used with any meeting rules or polity.

Discernment is said to have occurred when a decision is taken. When that decision is taken with the highest level of consensus among the decision-makers, then it is more likely, as per a strong Protestant theological tradition, to be aligned with the will of Christ for his church. It is also a decision that will have the strongest possible support from the group, and as such will be better supported outside of the meeting.

A decision needs to be documented. It should be clear to anyone who was not at the meeting what was decided, who will take responsibility for the implementation of the decision, and any next steps that will flow from the decision.

In some contexts it will be appropriate to have a formal conclusion to the process, for example, prayer or liturgical action or a celebration.

STEP 4: IMPLEMENT THE DECISION.

In this step, it's time to make the decision known in the community and to implement it. A decision is only of any use if it is put into effect. People who are affected should be assisted to understand and work with it. When decisions are shared openly with the people impacted by them they are respected and supported and the community's life is healthier.

Strategies that foster healthy community life include the following:

- sending a letter to the congregation and key leaders, sharing the details of the decision
- thanking people for their prayer and affirming why this decision is right for the church
- requesting ongoing prayer for the implementation of the decision
- using websites, church notices, announcements, worship services, and so on to respond to the feelings, hopes, and concerns of the community
- assessing the process with key leaders; sharing your experience of the meeting and discussing what went well and what could be improved.

Ensure that the final decision includes clear lines of accountability, which makes it clear who is responsible for what tasks, the date by which they must be completed, and any expectations with regard to reporting back.

Reporting on the actions that follow on from decisions is an essential element in building confidence and trust in the process. Clearly some actions are very simple. More involved pieces of work may take time and require a number of supplementary decisions. Many an act of discernment has been undone because no one had responsibility to see that the decision was implemented. A good discernment process will build in monitoring, reporting, and accountability systems so that a faithful act of discernment bears the fruit that the Holy Spirit intends.

Build into the process a time for reflecting on the process and identifying ways to improve it.

CONCLUSION

In the movie *Pirates of the Caribbean: At World's End*, there is a fascinating scene. The ship and crew are stuck in a purgatory-type existence in which they cannot sail or take on fresh provisions. They are hungry, exhausted, and dying. The pirate, Jack Sparrow, looks at their map one more time to see if there is a way to get out of their miserable existence. With the flick of his hand he turns the middle of the map around, and the solution becomes obvious: down is up! The way out of their situation is to rock the boat until it flips. Without a word he begins running from side to side looking over the side with a curious remark. People join him. Suddenly the large ship is rocking and flips. Sunset occurs. Did they do the right thing or just scuttle their ship? With a big whoosh, the boat begins to rise and flips right side up. When they open their eyes they see a beautiful sunrise and know they are saved.

It often takes courage to try something new. You may be wondering if it's worth it to try an alternative decision-making process in your congregation or organization. In short: yes, it is! Yes, you will need to train people and get their support. Yes, this approach disempowers those in your group who know how to use *Robert's Rules of Order* to get their way. Yes, it will be different. Yes, all these things are worth it if you are concerned about your congregation or group in the long run. We believe that congregations and groups that try this approach are stronger because of it. We know that this process fundamentally shifts the question to be considered from "what do we want?" to "what does God want of us?" It is time for a shift in the way we make decisions. And like Esther in the Old Testament, the job falls to you to make a stand. Be courageous!

John Wesley is attributed to have given this prayer to his Methodist Circuit Riders to encourage and focus their attention on God's mission:

Fix thou our steps, O Lord,
that we stagger not at the uneven motions of the world,
but go steadily forward—never ceasing the journey
for weather or stepping out the way for anything else that befalls us.[1]

---

1. Veronica Zundel, ed., *Book of Famous Prayers* (Grand Rapids: Eerdmans, 1983), 64.

When you think of your congregation or organization, are you moving steadily forward in God's mission by focusing on discerning God's will together?

DISCERNMENT AS A COMMUNITY ACTIVITY

Gathering as a faith community using a consensus-building approach to decision-making is only one part of the process. For that part of the process to work well it requires that participants be well prepared long before they get to the meeting. A consensus-building approach is part of a longer movement of preparation. When invited into the process with respect and trust, people eagerly look forward to participating in making a good decision together. When the destination of discernment is reached, it needs to be recognized that not everyone affected is present in that place. People who were outside the meeting need to be helped to own the decision and to share the excitement and confidence of those who have been charged with leadership. They need to be supported in this with well-constructed communication and other actions that bring them to the same place as those who made the decision. The ability of people to accept major decisions will be significantly enhanced by the extent to which they are invited into the preparation for discernment, and are communicated with after they receive the decision.

Discernment is only the first part of faithfulness. Knowing what Christ wants for his church is one thing. Doing it is another. Therefore any discernment process must ultimately lead to faithful action in response to the decision that has been made.

REFLECTION QUESTIONS

1. Which of the four parts of the cycle do you use the most in your context?

2. Which part(s) can you employ more than you do at present?

3. Can you think of a situation in which the failure to use all parts of the cycle had a detrimental effect? Discuss it with the

group that has responsibility for planning meetings in your organization.

ACTIVITY: TRIPLE RECALL BIBLE STUDY

This activity is helpful to use as you begin your decision-making process. It prepares the group for the matter before them by allowing them space to consider God's will in the matter rather than just jumping into the proposal or legislation. Select an appropriate Bible passage or a reading from a book or the Web.

1. Before the meeting, make a handout of the scripture or reading for each participant.

2. At the meeting, distribute the handouts to people.

3. Explain the process:

   a. Explain to participants that they will hear the reading three times. After each reading they will be given a question to reflect upon.

   b. Reading #1: After the first reading, there will be a pause to reflect on the material. Specifically: "What word or phrase lingers after this reading?"

   c. After three minutes, invite individuals to pair with another and share their responses with each other.

   d. Reading #2: After the second reading, there will be a pause to reflect on the material. Specifically, "What does this reading say about being a disciple of Jesus Christ?"

   e. After three minutes, invite individuals to gather into small groups of four to share their responses with one another. Invite a person from each group to share with the total group what was said in their small group.

   f. Reading #3: After the third reading, there will be a pause for individuals to reflect upon what this reading might say to their church/religious organization today.

g. After three minutes, invite people to share their responses with the total group. Record comments on newsprint or white board.

h. You can use this response sheet to assess whether you have discerned the will of God after the decision has been made by calling people back to it.

Sample Passages include:

Matthew 23:23
John 17:20-23
1 Corinthians 1:10-12
2 Corinthians 5:16-21
Romans 14:17
Ephesians 4:26 and 5:21
Philippians 2:1-11
Colossians 3:9 and 15

ACTIVITY: MY SMALL-GROUP LISTENING SHEET

My Small-Group Listening Sheet

Proposal (or Issue for Decision):

Why is this matter important to us?

What are the goals of our church/organization that relate to this issue?

Considerations that influence this decision:		
Listening and Discerning		
MY PERSPECTIVE	**PERSPECTIVE OF OTHERS**	**OUR BEST WAY FORWARD**

Preparation:

1. Begin by reading or sharing a brief presentation on the proposal. (This should be limited to ten to fifteen minutes.)

2. Form small groups of 6-8 people. Make these groups inclusive (gender, race, age, etc.).

3. Distribute the worksheet and explain that the purpose of the sheet is to support respectful listening and generate clear options to issues that affect ministry in your context. Review each section of the worksheet and explain its purpose:

   a. Proposal—This section names the specific issue under discussion. The sponsoring group words it. The proposal should be written so it is brief and understandable. Time should be given to a presentation with time for questions and answers.

b.   Why is this important to me?—This section can be done in the entire group and lists why you care about the issue.

c.   Goals of our church that relate to this proposal—This section names the specific goals that support the development of this option. The entire group should complete it.

d.   Considerations or questions that come to mind as you consider this proposal—this section is a running list.

e.   Listening

f.   My Perspective—use this section to record your best idea on this proposal. It may be a change to the petition or a hope.

g.   View of others—this middle area is to record the views of others in your small groups. Invite each person to participate in the discussion. Write a brief phrase to capture every person's ideas. They may be in support of the proposal or a change.

h.   Our Best Way Forward—have conversation on what idea best rises in support of your group in deciding the matter before them. Be succinct and record it.

i.   Notes—this section lists any additional information that is helpful to the group in deciding the matter before them.

Worksheet Instructions:

1.   Fill out the worksheet by completing the top section of the first page as a whole group.

2.   Complete the first column "My Perspective" individually (allow up to 10 minutes). Complete the second column as a group by allowing each person to voice their perspective. The third column documents the developing thinking of the group about the best way forward. Allow sufficient time to complete this task. It usually takes twenty to thirty-five minutes for simple proposals and thirty to fifty minutes for more complex matters. Remind people when they have five minutes to complete their small group work so they can accomplish the task.

3. Call the group together and invite each group to take turns shar-
    ing their "clear choice."

Provide enough time for questions and answers after each presentation.

List the proposal and various options on a separate piece of paper. Give
each person ten stickers and ask them to vote for their best options. They may
choose to place ten stickers on one option that they favor or split them up
among the options they can support.

Have a volunteer count the stickers and place the votes for that option
in a circle.

Write the best option on a clean sheet of newsprint with room below it
for notes.

Invite the group to receive recommendations for the following:

1. Decide on who is responsible for implementing the decision. By
    when?

2. Is there funding necessary to implement the change? If so, who
    will make a budget?

3. Responsible group

Conclude the activity with a prayer circle or sing a hymn.

CHAPTER 6

"YES, BUT..."

Addressing Resistance

Jesus was very sure on the idea of trusting God for what we need in order to fulfill our calling as disciples. There is the well-known example of the disciples being told to take no moneybag or spare shirt as they go on their evangelical mission (Luke 9:1-3 and 10:1-4). It is easy to get the impression that Jesus just wants us to wander off without any thought to the challenges that lie ahead. However, Jesus does not want us to wander off indifferently into the challenges that face us in the life of discipleship, but rather to know that the way we will be able to meet those challenges is not through our own strength alone.

In another story, Jesus is reported as having a conversation that tells people to be realistic about the challenges that can arise for a person who chooses to follow him. Jesus encourages people not to be naive about the obstacles that will be in their path. What person who is building a tower does not first stop to consider all the costs involved and whether he has the resources to complete the task? Who, when faced by an enemy, does not consider whether he has the ability to overcome that enemy notwithstanding the odds that are against him (Luke 14:28-32)?

If you are convinced that the church is crying out for a new way of discerning the will of God for its life together, then you are not alone. If you believe that we can have genuine Christian fellowship even as we wrestle with matters of great importance about which we have different, passionately held positions, then you are correct. We encourage you to take this journey seriously.

As you embark on this important journey, we know that not everyone will agree with you. You may also have your own doubts about whether a community-affirming, collaborative, respectful, consensus-building process is viable. Some people question whether such a way of corporate discernment can work in the real world. It is time to take the advice of Jesus seriously and take stock of the challenges. Let us consider the objections that have been raised about the model of discernment that has been advocated in this book. Like the tower builder, we need to weigh what we are up against. Like the disciples sent on an evangelistic mission, we can also trust that God will provide all the resources that we need to fulfill the tasks that have been given to us to accomplish.

THE POWER OF CULTURE

Volumes of books have been written on what needs to be taken into account when organizations want to make radical changes to the way that they operate. We all know that there is more to changing the way a group operates than just moving the chairs into a different arrangement. It is beyond the scope of this book to offer a thesis on theories of organizational change. Nevertheless, it is important to acknowledge how hard it is to change the behavior of any group. If you decide that you will lead for change toward another way of discernment in your church, or a decision-making body within the church, then you are encouraged to carefully review chapter 2 again. You may also want to read some introductory texts on organizational change.

At this point it is worth mentioning how powerful the culture of your organization will be in determining how much acceptance there will be for a consensus-building process. Unless you are from a culture or organization that already uses a consensus approach to discernment, then you are operating in a culture that values many things that are at odds with the norms of a consensus-building approach. That culture will not step aside for a newcomer without a fight. There is an old saying that culture eats strategy for breakfast. Basically, we can have all the best ideas in the world, but unless we deal with the culture of the organization, then these new ideas will never survive. However, when new ideas can be linked to some aspects of the dominant culture, huge changes in practice are not only possible but also probable!

In the following pages, a number of the objections to the use of a consensus-building approach to discernment will be considered. On the surface, these objections present as simple matters of fact: Does this work? What about X, Y, and Z? Responses to these objections will be offered at the factual level. However, it is necessary also to be alert to the values and cultural forces that have given rise to these objections. Sometimes it will be necessary to dig a bit deeper into what is driving the objections so that the discussion can move to a deeper level.

When attention is given to the possible motives for opposition, a constructive conversation is usually possible. Change can happen. Reasons for resisting change are not always bad. They may reflect long held and valued principles, which are worthy of respect. Also, there will be times when the assumptions that give rise to the objections just have to be resisted as not being as valid as the proponents of them suggest that they are.

Systems develop equilibrium. They seek stability. Churches are no different to any other group in that they reach a point at which there is a power balance and the practices and attitudes of the group support that equilibrium. When change happens in a group then this equilibrium is unsettled. The first instinct of most groups is to reorient themselves to the familiar pattern of life, to restore the equilibrium, to return to the way things used to be. However, sometimes the imbalance created by the new situation is so great that it is not possible to go back to the old way.

Between the time when the equilibrium of a group or system is first unsettled until the time that a new balance is found—with different power relationships and culture and practices to support them—there is resistance. The people and groups that have had power and influence in the old system normally don't give it up easily, and so they push back hoping to restore the old systems of authority.

Moving away from the parliamentary style to a more collaborative, multi-faceted, community-based consensus approach will most likely upset the equilibrium of your group. Expect it! Be under no illusions that the people who benefit under the current system will be aware that they will lose power and influence under another system. For the most part they will not like this reality and so they will resist any change. Many of the objections that are raised to consensus-building discernment are because the people who have power under the current system don't want to lose it. A new process will change the power balances, and there will be new attitudes and practices required in order to sustain the new equilibrium. Expect that there will be people who will lose out in any changes. Expect that there will be a significant number of people, and the organization itself, who will be the beneficiaries of a new way of making decisions.

So what can go wrong?

Any human process can work well or poorly. No system is perfect, and that is true of the various styles of consensus-building decision-making. Therefore it is quite right and necessary to ask hard questions of the new consensus-building approach to ensure that it can deliver on what it promises, and, further, that helpful adjustments can be made to accommodate different contexts. So, let's get started on exploring the objections that have been raised about the consensus approach as a way of working through differences, and so seek opportunities to reach a place of discernment.

1. THE PROCESS TAKES TOO MUCH TIME!

The basic principles of a consensus approach include the following:

- ensuring that every person who wants to speak will have the opportunity to do so

- starting the discussion by participants sharing what is important for them as they consider an issue; and not just saying how they feel about the words in the paperwork provided for the meeting

- allowing people to offer insights through telling stories, sharing emotions, being listened to carefully, receiving reflective comments to be sure they have been understood, and asking all the questions that they may have

- exploring new lines of inquiry that arise from the discussion to see if it might lead to new possibilities

Yes, these conversations take time, but it is time well spent. Think of it as an investment in affirming the value of all the members of the group, identifying the whole range of possible responses to an issue, living as an authentic Christian community, and building ownership of the final decision. Just because something takes time does not mean that it is not time well spent.

However, to address the specific criticism, any contentious piece of business takes time at a meeting. The more heated the debate, the longer the queue at the microphone and the more amendments or alternatives that are put to the group; and all these possible changes need to be addressed. Contentious matters always take time. The question is how best to use the time that is available.

From our experience, a consensus approach to decision-making does not necessarily take more time than the parliamentary style; and sometimes it is actually quicker. It can be faster because people collaborate to find solutions that meet the needs of other members of the group. It can be more efficient because it can quickly identify where there is agreement and where there is a need for more work; and the effort can be put into that conversation. Changes to the original wording can be agreed upon through less rigid procedures, which saves time in receiving and speaking to amendments. Also, when a group has a higher percentage of people who agree with the final decision, there is a lot less time spent revisiting an issue outside and inside the formal decision-making context. Experience shows that these decisions stick and have a high commitment to implementation. This can more than compensate for some perceived loss of efficiency.

There are concerns that there will not be enough time to get the business done when a decision-making group gets larger than a local church council or board or when a group is bigger than thirty people. Consensus-building processes, and the practices that support them, have been used in gatherings as large and diverse as plenary sessions of the World Council of Churches (three thousand people) and the World Communion of Reformed Churches (twelve hundred people). Churches in South Africa, New Zealand, and Australia use a variety of approaches to build consensus in their national and regional bodies that have hundreds of voting members. It can be done.

There is a misconception that because everyone's voice is respected and has a right to be heard, that every person in the meeting will actually want to speak. In the minds of some people who raise this objection is the image of hundreds of people lined up at microphones waiting to have their say. However, the reality is that just because a person is assured that his or her voice is important does not mean that he or she will elect to say anything in a plenary session. Many do not speak because their perspective has already been shared by others, and it is not necessary to repeat a point in order to show support for a particular polar opposite position in a debate.

109

There are many ways in which the voices of people can be heard and their views shared without lining up at a microphone. Techniques and business procedures are available and will be shared in chapter 8. Some options include use of table groups and a small-group process. Churches that use this approach will have members sit in groups at round tables during the plenary session along with people from outside their region or friendship group. From time to time opportunity is given to explore issues in this temporary community. For some people, sharing in this context is sufficient assurance that they have been heard and their views considered. On occasions it assists them to articulate their views to the larger group, or they may be encouraged to do so by the other group members. If they don't feel able to speak publicly, another person at the table may offer to present their view for them. Some churches use a small- or community-group process as a way of building fellowship in larger meetings and of addressing complex business. In those settings people are heard, and those people can be heard without everyone having to hear what they have to say all at the same time. This saves a lot of time.

Perhaps the final observation to make on this objection is to note that not all items of business actually need a lot of conversation. Just as a meeting that has a parliamentary approach has formal business and items that don't attract much comment, the same is true for meetings that use other business practices. It is important not to assume that the time required for complex matters will be replicated across every piece of business. Having set the pattern for complex matters, a consensus-building approach flows through into the culture and so into how even simple business is handled.

2. IT ALL GETS TOO MESSY

Emotionalism takes over. People ramble and jump in at tangents. Making amendments is uncertain and can take place without people realizing that it has happened.

Robert's Rules of Order's claim to fame is that it is clear and predictable and allows things to be done decently and in good order. Anyone observing a church using consensus-building approaches might think that it has the look of a free-for-all. This impression is probably gained because it is not familiar and the processes are not understood. For most people, *Robert's Rules of Order* can look like a free-for-all with no obvious logic, with its amendments and foreshadowed amendments, points of order, personal explanations, and so on. Anything that is new looks strange and usually a bit out of control. There are well-developed rules that manage and facilitate building consensus. It has an order, customs and practices, techniques, and rules, and they work. Yes, they only work as well as the chairperson of the meeting, but that is true for any business procedure.

The observation that if one lets the emotions genie out of the bottle there is no certainty about what will happen next needs to be taken seriously. Some people are able to express strong emotions in ways that can be received by others, and some cannot. Some people will springboard off a comment in the discussion into places that seem to be totally unconnected and irrelevant. These can be challenging situations for many people. When this happens it can create discomfort and frustration for some participants. These are real responses to unfamiliar actions, and they have to be respected and handled well.

The first step when there is a significant expression of emotion—or what appears to be a strange tangent type of comment—is to ask oneself, "What is this person saying?" "How can I listen well to him so his perspective can be included in our deliberations?" These are opportunities for deep listening and inclusion. Questions for clarification are crucial. A person skilled in reflective listening might provide feedback to the contributor what they think she or he is saying. It is important for people not to allow their fear of the emotions of others to prevent them from listening deeply.

The gathered community, perhaps assisted by the presiding officer or chair, can assist by helping the person express himself or herself in another way, or by clarifying the point. If the emotions are actually out of control, then there is the opportunity for pastoral care. Care might be offered by people nearby or through prayer from the chair. When we invite people to be themselves because the community values them, there is always the possibility that more will be unearthed than was expected. Your discernment process needs to be ready for this and not be afraid of it.

3. EMOTIONS, RATHER THAN GOOD THINKING, TAKE OVER AND SHAPE THE OUTCOME, DUMBING DOWN THE DEBATE

This is a very values-laden objection. Values are not a bad thing, and it is worth talking about them. In this statement intellectual rigor, logical argument, and reason are highly valued and affirmed. All these are very important in the discernment process of a Christian community.

The assumption is that they are the only tools that lead to insight and wisdom, and that to accommodate other means of learning and developing an understanding of God's will is not appropriate. Indeed, such a critique of consensus denigrates other methods that are used for developing insight and learning.

The enthusiasm of the western and western-influenced churches, for reason, logic, and intellectual rigor, and their antipathy to story and emotions as a way of discerning the will of God, owes more to the culture of the Enlightenment and the Age of Reason than it owes to the witness of the scriptures. The first council of the church that we know of is the Council of Jerusalem. It was convened to discern whether God required that Gentile Christians must adhere to Jewish religious laws and in particular to the requirement for circumcision. The process of discernment that is reported in Acts 15:1-18 includes several places where Peter, Paul, and Barnabas tell stories of the work that God is doing among the Gentiles, where the experiences of the members of the gathered group, as well as reference to scripture, are drawn upon as a basis for insight, and where reasons are offered for taking a particular course of action.

Reason and theological arguments are important, and a consensus-building approach gives as much space for these positions to be advanced as any other contribution that people want to make. However, as the experience of the early church and the Bible make clear, scripture, tradition, stories, and experience are relevant for discerning the will of God.

The processes for discernment that are being advocated in this book are highly consistent with the way in which the scriptures show that discernment takes place. John Wesley encouraged Christians to practice discernment in their daily lives so that their words and actions would be aligned, to the best of their ability, to God's will. His methodology is known as the Wesley Quadrilateral, which is the four reference points to help a person navigate a course for discerning God's will. The reference points are, as in Acts 15, scripture, tradition, reason, and experience. Far from being an intrusion, experience—shared through stories and emotions—is indispensable to discerning the will of God.

Not only does this objection fly in the face of the experience of the early church, and the tradition of John Wesley, but also it is fundamentally out of step with the norms of many cultures. Native American, Aboriginal Australian, Pacific Island, Asian, and other cultures do not resonate with *Robert's Rules of Order* as a culturally natural fit for how decisions should be made. There is no justification for asserting that these cultures have nothing important to teach the western church about how to discern the will of God. To say so is at best arrogant and at worst racist.

The feminist critique of power and authority in the context of how decisions are made has been advanced for many years. Thankfully the increased presence of women in leadership in many churches has helped some churches realize the privilege that has been given to men in the structures and practices of the church. Women in the church, and in society more widely, want a more collaborative and gentle style of decision-making. This gender-based insight should be taken seriously, not least because women make up more than 50 percent of the members of most churches, although sadly not over 50 percent of the leadership in many churches. God has gifted women for leadership in the church. It is therefore imperative that the way the church engages in corporate discernment is one that honors the insights and ways of thinking that are meaningful for women and not just for men. It should be noted that the desire for this kind of alternative community practice is not limited to women, as there are many men who share the same desire.

Some men like the parliamentary style of decision-making. A parliamentary style of decision-making favors people who are intellectual, linear thinkers who have a good grasp of reason and debating technique. When the executive of the then World Alliance of Reformed Churches met in 2009 to consider adopting a discernment process based on inclusiveness, collaboration, and empowerment of other voices and experiences, the first three speakers in the debate were all ordained men from northern European churches. Their objection was that the approach would give too much place for emotions and dumb down the debates. They liked the current system because they were good at it and knew how to make it work for them. I am not ascribing base motives to their objections, but the fact was that a new meeting process would share the power and they would lose influence in the meeting. While more people were gaining a voice, they were not losing their voice. They were still at liberty to bring their particular perspective to the deliberations. Their power may be weakened, but their participation remained; and they were not turned into victims. Once some women and some people from non-western cultures spoke in the meeting, the direction of the discussion changed and the new business procedures were approved.

4. CONSENSUS LEADS TO THE LOWEST-COMMON-DENOMINATOR DECISION

This objection is using the word *consensus* to describe the way a decision is taken, that is to say, by unanimous agreement. Consensus decision-making in this objection is used in contrast to making decisions by a vote, or through decision of a small group, or arbitration. Consensus is a decision-making method that is used in some churches.

However, this book is talking about consensus as a process for discernment, a way of being in community while seeking to discern the will of God. This is a different understanding of consensus because it focuses on the attitudes, practices, and processes that take place prior to the making of a decision. With this understanding of consensus one can use consensus processes but still allow for the possibility that having gone through this process a decision will be taken by a vote, by decision of a bishop, or by some other method of making a decision other than by consensus.

The process that is advocated in this book uses the self-description "consensus-building" because of the view that if a church group is seeking to discern the will of God, and since God only has one opinion on a subject, it should be our goal to find that one mind and agree to it as one. While that may be the theological affirmation and the hope of faith, there are times when decisions need to be taken by means other than consensus. Notwithstanding this reality it is still appropriate to seek discernment through consensus-based approaches.

5. THE CHURCH WILL LOSE ITS PROPHETIC VOICE

This objection is similar to the previous one but addresses the concern about how a large group of people can adopt a resolution that calls forth a prophetic position, when by definition such a voice is a minority in the church.

Noting that, as with the previous objection, this objection understands consensus as a way of making a decision, a brief comment is still in order.

The concern here is that unanimity, or near unanimity, is far less likely to be prophetic than using traditional rules for decision-making. There is little—if any—available evidence that prophetic statements by churches are more likely to be made with a slim majority than by unanimous decision. Is it reasonable to assume that a decision is more likely to be prophetic if it is made by a slim majority than unanimously? There are many examples of church bodies that seek consensus for their decisions but still have a reputation for being prophetic in their statements, or at least well ahead of the opinions of their members and society at large. Examples include the World Council of Churches, the Religious Society of Friends (the Quakers), and the Uniting Church in Australia.

These groups are listening to all the voices, generating alternatives that will assist more people in supporting the decision, and working together to discern the will of God. When all that work has been done and the position—however contentious the issue—is ready for determination, there is one more unique step that is available to a church that makes decisions by consensus.

In the parliamentary style it is almost expected that people will vote against something if they haven't been convinced to change their mind. In fact, it can seem weak not to be willing to vote with the minority right until the bitter end. Going to the mat for an issue, as the saying goes, is seen as a sign of courage and a badge of honor; she or he stuck to her or his principles no matter what!

In contrast, a consensus-building approach has a higher principle than sticking to what we, as individuals, think on a given topic. The principle that matters most in this alternative discernment process is the principle that the community of faith, prayerfully gathered and working together, is better placed to discern the will of God. When this principle is paramount there is no honor in resisting the wisdom of the vast majority and voting against something to the bitter end. Rather, the honorable thing to do is to defer to the wisdom of the whole group and stand aside to allow a decision to be taken. Churches and groups that seek to build consensus create a culture of collaboration that includes expressions of humility in which people don't fight tooth and nail to the bitter end, but willingly support the group even when its view is different to their personal preference.

Some might ask whether such things can ever happen. When the norms and culture of a group change from self-confident, combative, and oppositional to humble, collaborative, and team-building then people change the way they behave. Yes, it can and does happen.

6. A SMALL FRINGE GROUP CAN IMPOSE A VETO ON TAKING ACTION

Once again this objection has most substance when considering consensus as a way of making a decision. People who seek to prevent the group from making a decision can be a problem. A consensus approach places a high value on listening sensitively to minority voices. Even so, consensus processes do have ways to proceed in the face of people whose resistance to moving on is based more on a political strategy of obstructionism rather than a genuinely held belief. It is the experience of consensus-seeking churches that this emergency measure is rarely needed. The changed culture of the church makes it highly unlikely that people engage in obstructionist behavior.

7. CAN WE TRUST THIS PROCESS?

Just what part of the process one might not trust will, no doubt, vary among the people who raise this objection. The part of the process that most frequently raises a concern for people when they first come across this alternative process is the role of the facilitation team. This is a small group that receives the reporting sheets from the small-group discussions and then reports to the plenary on what has been received and provides advice on the next steps to take based on the feedback that has come from the small groups. This group goes by different names, but here the term *facilitation team* will be used in order to emphasize that it does not have an independent function. Rather it seeks to serve the whole meeting by helping it to hear what is being said in the small groups and then facilitating the meeting to find the way forward by offering specific suggestions.

Not every business meeting will use a small-group process; but when it is used, it is essential that the work done in the groups has a real opportunity to influence the direction of the meeting. For this to happen the comments from the small groups need to be processed. On occasion objections have been raised that there is scope for abuse because the members of the facilitation team could be partisan and write their preferences into the report and recommendations.

The recruitment of the most appropriate, spiritually mature, and trusted four or so people to serve the meeting in this way is the best strategy for dealing with this objection. The persons chosen must be people who are known to be able to put aside their personal positions for the sake of serving the church. They will be leaders who have the respect of the meeting and who have good process skills, orderly minds, creative insight, and good drafting skills.

Experience shows that it is not easy to pull the wool over the eyes of members when a facilitation team report comes back to a plenary session. People know whether what they are hearing makes sense. Furthermore there is the opportunity to ask questions of the facilitation team and to receive formally its report. So if there is a serious misreading, or an improper attempt to mislead the group, it will be found out at that point. Also, the new proposals for action that come from the facilitation team still have to be discussed, so there is no power in it to force its will onto the meeting. The confirmation of the faithful work of the facilitation team will be provided when the motions they bring back are put to the meeting, because if they have read the meeting correctly there should be strong support for what they have brought forward.

No system is free from manipulation. However with persons of the right character and skills selected to be on the facilitation team, and the opportunity for the meeting to review the work of the Facilitation Team when it presents its report, high levels of trust are possible.

8. WE'VE ALWAYS DONE IT THIS WAY

This is a tricky one and is included as a bit of a catchall to gather up a variety of concerns that have the common thread of fear of something new. Change should not be assumed to be easy. Most of us like what we know; and the older we get, the less appealing it is to change our ways! Notwithstanding this general truth, for the people of God it is not possible to stay with what has worked in the past if it is no longer effective today.

It is not uncommon for people to assess whether something is acceptable by how familiar it is with what they know. So, some people might reject a consensus approach because they do not recognize enough of the trappings of *Robert's Rules of Order*. A possible way forward with some of those people might be to point out the similarities even though they may look a bit different. For example, there is nearly always a form of words (whether they are called petitions, legislation, overtures, or proposals, etc.) to get things started; these can be changed and can be worked on in plenary sessions or in smaller groups (whether called legislative committees, sections, small groups, or working groups); and a decision will be made (most likely using a very familiar method).

While drawing attention to operational similarities between *Robert's Rules of Order* and consensus-building approaches will help some people, there is more impact by exploring the common values and goals that exist between the high aspirations of the old and the new. In doing so it is possible to note how both *Robert's Rules of Order* and the new process have respect for protecting a person's right to speak, ensuring that all points of view are heard, and ensuring that people are clear on what is being discussed and decided. These all continue to be affirmed. Yet the point also needs to be made that the new process is designed to support sound values in a way that the old rules do not. Appealing to what people value about the old, and from their Christian tradition, is an important way to assist people in making a change. It isn't all discontinuity from the past. In fact, the new process may well resonate much more strongly than the old process with significant values that people hold, once they are drawn out and highlighted.

For some people, a concern about leaving the traditional method of making decisions may reflect that they are afraid of where the Holy Spirit might lead. There can be confidence that familiar tracks lead to familiar destinations; but letting anyone have a say in a meeting may mean that there will be a change in the outcomes and directions for the organization. It may not be fear of a new process that gives rise to objection from some people, but a recognition that a new process may lead to a new outcome; and this is what makes the change scary! This requires that people receive the pastoral and spiritual support that they need in order to face change.

CONCLUSION

Before commencing to build a tower, the wise person takes time to assess whether she or he has the resources to complete the task. The purpose of this chapter is not to make the task seem harder but to resource you to complete the task by considering some of the objections we have heard.

Yes, there will be objections raised. It will simply not do to try to over-power them with force of will or political power. Deal with them carefully. As you enter into dialogue with people around their objections, do so in the spirit and with the tools of consensus-building. Listen carefully to be sure you understand their concerns, and let them know that you have heard them. Identify what you want to build together, and show how this approach can honor what is important to them as well as to you. Assume good will and a genuine desire in others to find ways that make it possible for the community of faith to together discern the will of God for this time and place. Model consensus-building and you will offer a credible witness to this alternative process of Christian discernment.

REFLECTION QUESTIONS

1. As you have reviewed the objections to consensus seeking, which ones have you encountered, and how would you respond now?

2. Are there any misgivings that you have even after reading this chapter? If so, contact the authors at the e-mail address provided on page 180.

3. How have you successfully introduced change? How can you use these learnings to introduce consensus in your congregation or organization?

LESSONS FROM AROUND THE WORLD

Across the world, churches are becoming increasingly dissatisfied with the traditional western ways of decision-making. For many the parliamentary style of business meetings is a colonial imposition that sits uneasily with their practices and assumptions about how wisdom is shared and insights are gained. For international ecumenical bodies, the situation is not only about cultural dissonance but also how to handle significant ecclesiological differences that are founded on long-standing and deeply held theological understandings. For those churches from western liberal democracies, the desire for change comes from the experience that decisions made in the old ways are often destructive for the communities in which those decisions are made.

This chapter provides examples from denominations and international ecumenical bodies that have developed a consensus-building approach to meetings.

A CHURCH THAT CHANGED THROUGH ITS DISCERNMENT PROCESS: THE EXPERIENCE OF THE UCA

Rev. Terence Corkin, General Secretary of the Assembly (2001–2015)

The Uniting Church in Australia (UCA) was inaugurated on June 22, 1977, through the union of the Congregational Union of Australia, the

Presbyterian Church of Australia, and the Methodist Church of Australasia. It is the third-largest church by affiliation at the national census. The UCA comprises nearly two thousand congregations and preaching places spread across Australia. It is a significant provider of education and community services, with over fifty schools that were commenced by the UCA or its predecessors, and it is the largest non-government provier of community services in Australia, providing aged care, and health and social services to more than two million people each year, or about one in twelve Australians.

About 8 percent of UCA congregations and faith communities are monocultural and non-English speaking. Also, there are significant numbers who are from another culture but worship in an English-speaking congregation. About 20 percent of the church's active membership and 15 percent of its ministers are from these culturally and linguistically diverse backgrounds.

When the UCA came into being, the three denominations all used fairly similar variants of the traditional parliamentary rules of debate. It soon became clear that even though the words in the rule books were similar, they had been interpreted differently in the various traditions. When churches joined the union many of their decisions were brought into question. There were many heated debates with vigor and passion in the first decades of the UCA.

By the fifth triennial meeting of the national Assembly (1988), there was recognition that the business procedures of the church needed review. A task group was set up whose membership comprised persons who knew the traditional rules of order very well and were also very comfortable with them.

The task group recognized that rules of order and meeting procedures are not an end in themselves. So before the task group started revising the standing orders, it reflected theologically on what people were doing when they made decisions in church meetings. It was affirmed that the goal of a decision-making meeting of a church council, committee, or board is to discern the guidance of the Spirit in response to the word of God. The new rules of order would express this commitment.

At the theological heart of the UCA's understanding of church government is that

- Christ is the head of the church

- Christ can and will lead people to faithfully serve his purposes

- God has gathered a community of called and gifted people with the responsibility to find Christ's will for his church in that particular context

These theological convictions require attitudes and practices that support them:

- **Christ is the head of the church**. This requires openness to new insights that Christ might bring (i.e., an attitude of humility and patience to get things done in God's time). A decision does not have to be popular. The church is not a democracy but a theocracy.

- **Christ can and will guide his people**. This requires trusting, taking time, and giving attention to the means of grace.

- **All possibilities have been considered**. Listen for surprising voices and ideas.

- **Allow all the issues to get put on the table.**

- **People are called and gifted to serve in this community of discernment**. All voices must be heard. This requires treating people with respect, understanding what is at stake for everyone, taking time, being prepared to reframe the discussion, working together to find a solution, building consensus as the process unfolds, and trusting that God can speak through someone with a different viewpoint from your own.

The task group then developed rules of procedure that supported these theological convictions and commitments.

The UCA process has three phases:

1. Introduction. Proposals are brought and the reasons for them are presented. This is followed by questions for clarification so that all members are clear on the intention of the proposal, the meaning of its words, and the implications of it being passed in its present form.

2. Deliberation. This is the most substantial phase and uses a variety of methods.

3. Determination. This is usually quick, as consensus has normally been achieved before a decision is sought.[1]

BEING OPEN TO THE LEADING OF THE HOLY SPIRIT

- At longer meetings, 20 percent of the time is set aside for worship and Bible study, in addition to any prayer that might be called for during the meeting.

- The process ensures that there is sufficient space in the agenda for all the theological, practical, pastoral, and other perspectives on an issue to be heard.

- Ecumenical guests are encouraged to participate in the discussions.

BEING A COMMUNITY SEEKING TO BUILD CONSENSUS IN DECISION-MAKING

- Time is spent building community. Without the community being well formed (worship is an important part of this process), discernment is much more difficult.

- The business before the meeting is called a proposal in order to convey the humility with which it is offered.

- Small groups are often used to involve everyone in the discussion.

- A "facilitation team" works to bring the insights from the small-group discussions back to a plenary session.

- Eight to ten members sit around each table. There is use of table group conversations within the plenary hall so people can think things through in a smaller group and be empowered to speak in the large group.

1. Interested readers can find more detailed information about "The Manual for Meetings" of the Uniting Church in Australia from the Assembly of the UCA website at assembly .uca.org.au/images/MfM2015.pdf. Hard copies are available from Mediacom at www.media com.org.au/.

- Colored cards are used to indicate whether there is support for a proposal or an amendment without it being a final determination.

- Even if there is only one person who is unable to support a proposal, that person will be heard.

- People can speak more than once if they consider that their view has not been understood or if they have something new to say.

- Proposals are changed as the meeting proceeds without the need for formal amendments, where support for such a change is identified through the use of the indictor cards.

- There is a clear flow in the business from introduction and clarification of the issues through the deliberation phase and then to a determination.

SOME REFLECTIONS ON THE IMPACT OF CONSENSUS DECISION-MAKING IN THE UCA

Rev. Gregor Henderson served as General Secretary of the Assembly of the UCA (1988–2000) and as President (2006–2009). He was on the Central Committee of the World Council of Churches for two terms and was Discernment Advisor at the 2013 Busan Assembly and at meetings of Central Committee since 2006.

Meetings of the Uniting Church have a very different feel about them these days because of the church's shift to consensus decision-making. Some of the main changes are:

(a) There's a much greater sense of common purpose among members. People are not out to win the day but are generally committed to discerning the best way forward together.

(b) There's much less sense of factionalism. People are not categorized into boxes so easily, as there's a greater openness to hearing differing viewpoints and to changing your position.

(c) Respectfulness toward people of different views and from different backgrounds is far greater. Minority groups such as members from non-Anglo backgrounds and indigenous members, or those with a particular theological emphasis, are no longer squashed. People are listened to far more readily than before. Hostility has virtually disappeared from our church meetings.

(d) It's a more spiritual and prayerful ethos. In the best of our consensus debates you can feel the movement of the Holy Spirit as the colored indicator cards show members' immediate reactions to speeches, as the President summarizes the flow of the discussion or leads in prayer, and as the whole meeting moves toward a consensus.

Especially in tense and highly charged debates our consensus procedures have proven to be a gift and blessing to the church.

Consensus has brought change, not just to our major church meetings, but to the church as a whole. Deep differences of opinion tend to be resolved at the meeting and are far less likely now to end up with resentment or long-standing animosity. The old way of decision-making tended to leave people feeling bruised and hurt. Different viewpoints were tolerated at best. Now we reach decisions that accept that there are different viewpoints. Acceptance that there is diversity among church members is now the norm.

Dr. Jill Tabart is a medical practitioner who was a participant in the task group that developed the Manual for Meetings and was President of the Assembly (1994–1997). Jill has been an advisor and mentor on consensus-building processes for the World Council of Churches and the World Communion of Reformed Churches.

I am passionate about the benefits to the church community that have been our experience in the UCA since we changed our meeting procedures. When it's done well we see the following qualities:

- We mutually recognize that all are gifted by God; so all have a contribution worthy of respect.
- There is increased listening to one another so that all are genuinely seeking the best way forward for the church. Even those

with strong views are able to acknowledge wisdom in another's point of view and work together to adapt the wording of a proposal toward a wiser outcome.

- Proposals are developed progressively through discussion, using strategies such as small-group conversations, pauses for prayer, and time out for musing over morning tea.

- We have a greater awareness of our need to wait on the guidance of the Holy Spirit. Under former procedures there were many who doggedly persisted until they could "win" a majority with their predetermined point of view uninfluenced by any other contribution.

- Voices of those previously disadvantaged in meetings are heard. In our church, that would be women, indigenous members, young people, those for whom English is not their first language, and those unfamiliar with standing orders and inexperienced in the cut and thrust of vigorous debate.

- The use of colored cards indicate warmth or coolness to another person's point of view. This seemingly simple means of expressing a response allows each member (even those for whom standing to speak at a microphone will always be too daunting) to contribute to a meeting's overall discernment. It also ensures that the person chairing the meeting can quickly see where the mind of the meeting is developing.

- There is broader ownership of a decision. Where all, or nearly all, support a decision, participants are then better equipped to explain to the rest of the church the reasons why a particular decision was reached. When using parliamentary procedures, barely more than half those participating can determine an outcome, and the rest may go away saying, "It was someone else's choice, not mine."

The UCA has welcomed the more "user-friendly" meeting procedures. We have discovered that consensus decision-making is about a change of attitude. It is a change in heart and mind about what we are doing, and why, as we make decisions. The church overall is benefiting from that awareness and practice.

Rev. Eseta Waqabaca-Meneilly migrated from Fiji in 1988 as a minister of the Methodist Church in Fiji. She has served as Chairperson of the Maribyrnong Valley Presbytery (1995–1997), Chairperson of the meeting of heads of the national Assembly's multicultural National Conferences (1998–present), and member and Chairperson (2010–2012) of the Assembly's Multicultural and Cross Cultural Ministry Reference Committee.

In the Fijian culture, decisions are made in community. Men make decisions while sitting around a bowl of yaqona, the traditional drink, and women sit around a cup of tea and biscuits. The men usually have these meetings in the evening, the women during the day. These meetings go on for as long as they need, ending only when a decision is reached. If no communal agreement is arrived at and family responsibilities are calling (for women) or sleep calls (for men), both groups will simply agree to leave the conversation at that point and pick it up again tomorrow. The next day before the meeting, one or two may approach the "disagreeing" component of yesterday's meeting and do some talking or negotiating. This usually would be a close friend or relative. The meeting continues the next day, and the next if needed. But if on the agreed last day the meeting runs out of time, a majority of voters will decide the outcome.

I recognize the UCA decision-making by consensus is the same mode of decision-making used by people in Fiji. Consensus is agreeing or disagreeing in community. Communal life, networks, relationships, and belonging are the foundations of all life and all of creation.

Consensus is biblical. The Triune God uses this mode of decision-making! Western-trained minds sometimes hear communal conversations as a waste of time and a loss of individual identity, an inability to make choices or make decisions without the approval of others. An individualist doesn't have to take the matter to community.

Western individualism sits uneasily with Fijian culture. We make decisions together and take the time required to reach, as often as possible, a shared understanding of what the decision should be. A consensus-building approach to decision-making is more attuned to Fijian and other Pacific cultures.

CONCLUSION

The UCA has twenty years of experience with its consensus-based approach to decision-making. The church seeks to build consensus (a methodology through which its deliberations take place) and also to make its decisions by consensus (the method by which a matter is determined). The decision to operate in these two ways has had a profound effect on the meeting practices of the UCA. It has had a life and character-transforming effect on the kind of community that is the Uniting Church.

BUILDING CONSENSUS IN AFRICA: THE UNITING PRESBYTERIAN CHURCH IN SOUTHERN AFRICA

The Rev. Dr. George Marchinkowski is Past Moderator of the Uniting Presbyterian Church in Southern Africa (UPCSA), and Business Manager for the Assembly.

In March 2005, the Uniting Presbyterian Church in Southern Africa (UPCSA) decided to explore alternative ways of making decisions in its General Assembly. This arose as a result of growing discontent with the Westminster system, which had been used by the church since its inception in 1897. The UPCSA consists of nineteen Presbyteries across three countries: South Africa, Zimbabwe, and Zambia. A working group was formed that visited the Uniting Church in Australia to study its consensus processes and to assess whether these would work in an African context. In February 2006, consensus processes were observed in action at the World Council of Churches meeting in Porto Alegre, Brazil.

In September 2006, the UCPSA experimented with procedures for decision-making based on the Uniting Church in Australia's system in its biennial General Assembly. Since then, the system has been used on many occasions in meetings of the General Assembly and Executive Commission. Some Presbyteries have adopted versions of it in their meetings. Based on these experiences, some conclusions can be drawn about the consensus model and its use.

129

THE IMPORTANCE OF KNOWING THE ROLE OF THE DECISION-MAKING BODY

One of the important questions considered was the role of the General Assembly and what are its primary tasks. The UPCSA began to consider "celebration" and "discernment" as the assembly's primary work. Having discerned this purpose, the General Assembly became, first an occasion to notice what God is doing in our midst and for the church to thank God for God's generosity to the church and community.

The second purpose of the assembly is to discern. It was called to discern God's will in many areas.

The consensus system better equipped the assembly to accomplish its work. It called commissioners to act as members of a team seeking to discern God's will together.

THE SPEED WITH WHICH WE MAKE DECISIONS

One of the most controversial aspects of the consensus system was that it seemed to "slow down" the decision-making process by dividing it into three phases: listening, discussing, and deciding. The result is that an important proposal that previously took a few minutes to become a decision could now take several hours. Detractors argued that this would substantially reduce the amount of business the assembly could consider. In practice, by grouping reports and proposals, the assembly still manages to get through the same amount of business. The General Assembly has consistently completed its work and has not curtailed its agenda at all.

MOVING AWAY FROM WINNERS AND LOSERS

What we have discovered is that the consensus system achieves a greater buy-in for decisions in the assembly by intentionally building community among the members. The system achieves the creation of a greater sense of community by providing opportunities for worship and fellowship in the agenda, by placing members into small groups for discussion of proposals, and by encouraging fellowship over mealtimes.

In addition, it achieves a greater buy-in because it slows down the process of making a decision. By allowing more time, members of the council have a greater opportunity to understand the issues being proposed. The debate component of the parliamentary procedure is replaced by a holy conversation, in which each member contributes to the group's perspective on God's mind about a particular matter. This results in the members of the group owning the "developing opinion." By the time the proposal is put for decision, the proposal belongs to the whole body that has journeyed with it to this moment.

It is important to note that Presbyterian decision-making is, in its very nature, a communal exercise. The polity that John Calvin envisaged saw elders and ministers gathered as equals under the king and head of the church to transact the business of the church at every level. African culture also emphasizes communal decision-making. The Zulu concept of Ubuntu expresses personhood in a communal way. Ubuntu sees personhood as "collective interdependence." Desmond Tutu put it this way, "It is about the essence of being human.... We believe that a person is a person through other persons; that my humanity is caught up and bound up in yours...you seek to work for the common good because your humanity comes into its own in community, in belonging."[2] In the African worldview, none of us is greater than all of us. We need one another; there is an eternal bond of reciprocity between us. It is in a courageous encounter with others that we discover our common destiny. This is a radical departure from the Cartesian individualistic worldview prevalent in the West. It is implicitly collaborative and, therefore, welcoming toward a more consensual approach to discernment.

Also, we have found that it is much more difficult for a group of people who have journeyed long with a proposal to be persuaded by opportunistic argument, than it has been for a group that has just heard a proposal put for the very first time.

INCREASING PARTICIPATION

Whereas the Westminster parliamentary system has opportunity for debate in the plenary sessions, the consensus system includes discussion of a proposal primarily in small groups. Even critics of the system admit that this is one of the great strengths of the consensus model. First-time commissioners, who were cautious and reticent to make speeches before the

---

2. Desmond Tutu, *The Right to Hope: Global Problems,* Global Vision (1995).

General Assembly, readily contribute in a smaller (ten- to twelve-member) group. Over the course of the meeting the group meets and members get to know one another, so the quieter members begin more readily to offer their perspectives.

Speakers are encouraged to explore rather than argue in favor of or against. On many issues, there are multiple viewpoints, not just two. The group is charged with discovering together, in mutual submission, the will of God for the church on each of the issues before them. The rigid formal procedural environment created by the Westminster parliamentary system seemed to intimidate many new commissioners who didn't understand its rules, especially those who spoke English as a second language. It favors the opinions and rights of the individual, particularly those who understand and use the rules well. The consensus system favors the group and its collaborative task of discovering God's will on a particular matter. The less formal environment in the small groups encourages participation.

A CREDIBLE DEADLOCK-BREAKING MECHANISM

One of the places the UPCSA has struggled with the consensus system is the perception that it lacks a credible deadlock-breaking mechanism. The Westminster system very rarely has a deadlock. A proposal is usually carried or lost. The only time a deadlock can happen is when the vote is tied. Here the moderator casts the deciding vote and the deadlock is broken. In our consensus process, the moderator has no casting vote because votes are not taken.

A radical mind shift was required to adequately address the issue of a lack of a deadlock-breaking mechanism. The objective in this system is not to break a deadlock so that a decision will be made, but rather to gauge the ongoing consensus or lack thereof. If colored indicator cards are used, they should not be counted the same as hands or ballots are counted in the parliamentary system; rather it is the developing opinion of the meeting that is gauged. As commissioners work together to discover God's will, a consensus begins to form; and when it is fully formed, we have arrived. Therefore, the moderator, or chair of the meeting, asks questions such as: "Do you believe we have consensus in support of/not to support this proposal?" The commissioners indicate using their colored cards. If there is unanimity, then a decision is recorded.

If there is no unanimity, members of the council are called upon to deliberate further. The purpose of the discussion is not to persuade the minority but rather to mold the proposal into a decision. There is room for a lone prophetic voice and for telling stories about God's work in the church as this relates to the proposal. The moderator may use such questions as: "Do those who are unable to support the proposal believe that your point of view has been listened to and that the discussion has been fair, and will you allow the general mind of the meeting to be the decision?" If the minority gives consent, there is a decision by consensus. It should be kept in mind that the task of decision-making in the consensus system is communal and is not the sum of individual votes.

There are other options in the search for consensus. In the consensus process, the expression of a diversity of opinions can be a council's decision. We are finding more and more that the expression of a diversity of opinions may be a more honest approach than a decision that was made by a small majority and a large minority.

The consensus model of decision-making has credible ways of encouraging a council to move toward consensus. A council should not force commissioners toward consensus for the sake of recording a decision, but rather gently encourage them to seek the will of God together. Furthermore, a council has not been defeated when it cannot arrive at unanimity.

CONCLUSION

In 2003, the General Secretary of the World Council of Churches, Dr. Samuel Kobia, wrote: "Power is power, be it in governments, nongovernmental organizations or churches. The churches can genuinely raise their voices in a changing world only if they also decisively reform the hierarchical and partly undemocratic leadership structures in their own houses."[3] It has been our experience that reforming the decision-making processes of the church is part of a larger program of reform of structures that must take place before the denomination I serve can truly be an African church.

Dr. Kobia continues:

---

3. Samuel Kobia, *The Courage to Hope: The Roots for a New Vision and the Calling of the Church in Africa* (Geneva: WCC Publications, 2003), 167.

At the heart of this cosmology (the African worldview) is the principle of participation. It is this vision of interdependent participation that creates structures of inclusivity and hospitality that make life whole. It is through participation that the dignity of every individual is affirmed. To be is to participate. Exclusion from meaningful participation in matters that vitally affect one's life renders one a non-person.[4]

So the question is: Who must participate? Surely, we who belong to the church must all be offered the opportunity to participate at different times and in different ways. The project of the UPCSA has been to offer a method of decision-making that is more participatory, more hospitable, and more dependent on relationship. The consensus model met our needs.

Finally, Dr. Kobia warned: "Building a culture of participation is a long and slow process, but there could be urgent need for particular, immediate changes."[5] Indeed, the transition from making decisions with a Westminster worldview to discerning by consensus has been slow and challenging. It is difficult to unlearn a way of thinking. One of the greatest obstacles to the effective use of the consensus method has been that we began using this system with a Westminster worldview. This resulted in strange hybrids like the counting of colored indicator cards (which were never supposed to be counted!) and the temptation to debate when opportunity for dialogue and discussion is offered. The challenge of mastering our desire for a single final answer, so that we may embrace a situation in which a diversity of opinions exist, remains with us. Abandoning our desire to overwhelm minorities also remains a continuing goal. It is difficult to introduce something new without people feeling threatened.

A more consensus-based approach to corporate Christian decision-making is more appropriate in a context in which participation is encouraged. It makes room for the inexperienced participant, the tentative speaker, and the person who has not mastered the rules of the meeting, or even the English language. The system is concerned with the building of community because of the belief that the will of God in a particular matter is found in the midst of a community searching together in dependence on God for a way forward.

The consensus system has its problems, and perhaps most serious among these is its inherent idealism. The system works well where there is a strong,

---

4. Ibid., 191.

5. Ibid., 161.

cohesive, and hospitable community. But where does such a community exist? Our church community is, at its best, multicultural, multiethnic, broken, and searching; and at its worst, it is characterized by political infighting and posturing. This community has a broken past and huge socioeconomic challenges in the present. Does the consensus system work for an imperfect community like ours? We believe that the only way to design a system for a community is to design it aspirationally—for the community at its best—and then to design checks and balances to address the community at its worst. An aspirational design should seek to enshrine strong values in the system. We believe the consensus system has these. The checks and balances should include rules that assure fair treatment to all participants, and the curbing of the powers of those who administer and facilitate the system.

The consensus system, as we have experimented with it, has left us with many unanswered questions and a lot of development work to do. As with any living system, this one should probably be in a continuing state of development. If the values are strong, then the system will stand up to the challenges of our time and context. We believe this system will also contribute to the wider program of reform in the church, as the twenty-first century offers us new opportunities to understand ourselves as the Church of Jesus Christ in the world.

CONSENSUS DECISION-MAKING IN THE WORLD COUNCIL OF CHURCHES

Rev. Gregor Henderson, member WCC Central Committee (1998–2013), WCC Consensus Advisor (2013–2014).

The World Council of Churches (WCC) is a conciliar body consisting of representatives from more than 340 member churches. In 1948, when the WCC was established, it consisted almost entirely of Protestant churches from Europe and North America, for whom the long-standing "parliamentary" procedures of motions and amendments and voting were well known. By the 1990s, membership included Orthodox churches and churches from Africa, Asia, and Latin America. For these churches the old European parliamentary procedures were unfamiliar, complex, and problematic.

Concerns from Orthodox churches and a few Protestant churches were twofold: the theological conviction that there must be a better way of

determining an outcome than just by simple majority vote, and the prag-
matic concern that the minority churches could always be outvoted by the
Protestant majority on significant matters.

The WCC Assembly in Harare, Zimbabwe (1998), appointed a special commission "to study...issues related to Orthodox participation in the
WCC,...(and to) make proposals concerning the necessary changes in structure, style and ethos of the Council."

The Central Committee (2002) accepted the special commission's recommendations, and new rules were drafted and applied for the first time at
the Central Committee meeting in 2005 and the WCC Assembly in Porto
Alegre, Brazil in 2006.

There are several key factors in the new WCC model:

- Consensus is defined as all agreeing (unanimity) or most agreeing and the others accepting that their views have been heard
  and not objecting to the outcome.

- The theological basis for consensus is grounded in the principle
  that meetings are communities of faith in which participants
  together seek to discern God's will.

- Emphasis is on respectful listening to all points of view and
  genuine dialogue.

- Deliberate processes for ensuring business sessions are embedded in a context of Bible study and prayerfulness.

- The use of table group discussion is expanded.

- Indicator cards are used after speeches by delegates and when
  checking for consensus (orange is agree, and blue is disagree).

- Individual or church dissent from a decision can be recorded,
  as can abstention.

- If a member church's ecclesiological self-understanding is
  threatened by a prospective decision, then consideration of that
  decision will be deferred.

- Formal majority decision-making is retained for a few matters, such
  as amendments to the constitution, adoption of financial reports, and
  elections.

- Moderators for all WCC governing bodies are trained.

- A "Consensus Advisor" is appointed to assist the moderators at assemblies and central committee meetings.

- Orientation sessions on the new procedures are provided for all delegates.

- The procedures are evaluated and reviewed after each assembly.

The move to consensus was a very significant step in the life of the WCC. In his opening address to the WCC Assembly in 2006, His Holiness Aram 1, Catholicos of the Armenian Apostolic Church in Cilicia and Moderator of the WCC Central Committee from 1991–2006, said:

> The consensus model...is not only intended to change voting procedures;...it will promote participation, ownership and fellowship. Consensus...means preserving diversity and respecting differences and,...overcoming contradictions and alienation. Therefore, it is not merely a procedural matter; it is intended to challenge us to share our theological insights and spiritual experiences, as well as display our perspectives and concerns more effectively, empowering each other and seeking together the mind of the church....all member churches...constitute a fellowship and, therefore, are called to address issues in a non-confrontational way and in a spirit of mutual openness and trust.[6]

The official report of the Ninth Assembly (Porto Alegre, 2006) noted:

> Prior to the assembly, many delegates were haunted by the question of whether the consensus procedures would allow both for intense dialogue and the achievement of a common robust voice on key issues confronting the member churches of the WCC. At its conclusion, most people seemed inclined to answer the question affirmatively.
>
> A process of hearing distinct voices, while inquiring constantly about the reaction of the assembly, was respectful to the wide array of opinions and yet attempted to achieve a meaningful denouement. Debate took place, dissenting opinions were recorded, and decisions were achieved that proved satisfactory to most delegates.
>
> This, however, did not mean that everyone was entirely pleased. Voices

---

6. Report of the Moderator, WCC Ninth Assembly (Porto Alegre, 2006), WCC online resources, paragraph 24a, page 10. See http://www.oikoumene.org/en/resources/documents/assembly/2006-porto-alegre/2-plenary-presentations/moderators-general-secretarys-reports/report-of-the-moderator.

of dissent were heard and recorded on several matters, such as the restrictions on inclusive theological language and imagery in the activities of common prayer and the lack of attention, in the declarations, to divisive issues of human sexuality. Some delegates thought that the assembly's final declaration was fine as a prayer but that it was not truly a message because it did not make any reference to specific issues that were afflicting humanity, like the war in Iraq or the Israel-Palestine conflict. These were significant points of dissent.

However, the intention to be consensual prevailed while still allowing for dissident voices and ideas to be registered in the official documents.[7]

The overall response to the consensus model in the WCC has been very positive. There is, however, an ongoing concern among a few Protestant representatives that the WCC has lost some of its prophetic edge, as the consensus procedures can at times restrict the WCC from adopting strong "liberal" stances on current social and political issues.

I have no doubt the WCC has changed for the better through its new procedures. Its governance meetings are less adversarial and more deliberate in learning from different Christian perspectives and in building Christian fellowship. There's a greater sense of appreciation for what different Christian traditions bring to the table and much wider ownership of the decisions made. The active participation of representatives from Orthodox churches and churches from Africa, Asia, and Latin America has grown markedly. The WCC and the worldwide ecumenical movement are well served by the consensus model of decision-making.

TRYING FOR CHANGE—THE UNITED METHODIST GENERAL CONFERENCE 2016

Rev. Terence Corkin, Consultant on alternative decision-making processes to the Commission on the General Conference and facilitator for consensus-building in decision-making.

---

7. "God, in Your Grace" official report of the WCC Ninth Assembly, ed. Luis N. Rivera-Pagán (Geneva: WCC Publications, 2007), 42–43.

BACKGROUND

The United Methodist Church (UMC) is a transnational church of approximately eight million members originating in the United States, with a significant presence in many parts of Africa, the Philippines, and Europe. The church is governed by conferences. The General Conference is the meeting of delegates from across the world that occurs every four years to make decisions that guide its life and witness.

When the General Conference met in Tampa, Florida, in 2012 the vigor with which divergent opinions on the inclusion of homosexual people in the life of the church were expressed led to a great many delegates feeling hurt and shocked at the way Christians had dealt with one another. The delegates thought there had to be a better way to address deeply divisive issues. As a result the General Conference authorized the Commission on the General Conference (the body that prepares for the next meeting of the General Conference) to provide an alternative approach for decision-making for use at the 2016 General Conference in Portland, Oregon.

THE CHALLENGES FOR THE UMC

There were a number of factors that the commission had to take into account as it developed an alternative process. The most significant one was that any new process had to be able to be inserted into its normal business processes.

It was possible to design a process that could be accommodated within the decision-making processes of the General Conference. The process was a consensus-building approach that included a careful introduction of the issues and the process, with significant time available for questions for clarification, discussion questions that were designed for use in two structured small-group sessions, the completion of response sheets by the small groups in which their views on the petitions and any new ideas were documented, the use of a facilitation group to bring this information back to the plenary session in the form of a report and revised petitions based on the feedback received, and then deliberation of the report and new petition(s) using *Robert's Rules of Order*.

The Commission on the General Conference met the challenges of devising an alternative process that could be accommodated in their current system of decision-making, that was sufficiently different in that there was hope for a more constructive engagement around the issues; and to write a

Rule that could express a new business process (known as a Rule) that could express the alternative approach.

The UMC also faced the following challenges:

- recruitment of leaders for the small groups and the membership of the facilitation group
- training these leaders both before and at the venue of General Conference
- explaining the new rule to the delegates who would have to support it in a vote prior to it being implemented
- the significant lack of trust across the church in the structures and leadership of The UMC
- the highly politicized nature of groups around the issue on which the new rule would be used
- painful memories from the 2012 General Conference, where a different style of small-group process was used and was poorly received
- recognition by many people that they would not be as powerful if the new rule was adopted
- the need to translate significant amounts of material and to ensure that there were sufficient interpreters for multilingual groups

THE OUTCOMES FOR THE UMC GENERAL CONFERENCE

Web-based and on-site training was provided for the leaders in advance of the meeting. Everyone who participated in the training ended the experience with a very positive view that the process could make a different kind of conversation possible. Confidence grew as they understood the methodology and the principles that were behind the consensus-building approach that was being offered.

Many people had a sense that a respectful, honest, and community-building conversation was possible around a highly contentious issue in which emotions usually run high.

After much discussion the General Conference decided not to adopt the new rule. The alternative approach to decision-making was not implemented.

The sixty-seven petitions that were to be handled through the new rule were reassigned back to the legislative committee process and addressed in the normal manner. With respect to the core issue, the attitude of The UMC to the inclusion, or otherwise, of homosexual people in the life of the church, the meeting once again reached a stalemate. The bishops recommended that the General Conference authorize the Council of Bishops to establish a special commission on sexuality to study the matter and to bring recommendations back to the next General Conference (either 2020 or a called meeting in 2018).

DIFFICULTIES EXPERIENCED AND LESSONS TO BE LEARNED

The delegates to General Conference 2016 were not provided with pertinent information about the new rule that would allow them to raise informed questions or critiques of the process. This lack of vulnerability by the commission in the implementation process led to further suspicion and mistrust among the delegates. Many delegates were left with the impression that someone was trying to pull the wool over their eyes.

The silence of the official spokespersons left an information vacuum that was filled by persons and groups that were vehemently opposed to adopting the new procedure. Misinformation, misrepresentations, confusion, and suspicions were sown with no alternative narrative being provided by the commission's leadership.

People need a reason to change. Without a well-developed, principled, motivating, and coherently articulated rationale for trying something new, the tendency of groups, especially conflicted ones, is to revert to the status quo. The magnitude of the change being asked of the delegates in adopting a new rule cannot be overstated. Within this church's context there were few, if any, delegates who have done business other than by using a parliamentary process. This lack of firsthand knowledge meant that delegates had no personal reference points for what might be possible. Advocacy, if offered from the commission, through stories from other places, would have had a major effect in fostering openness to change.

This lack of planning extended to the small groups. For a variety of reasons, there were not sufficient leaders recruited for all the groups. There were going to be too many people in some groups, self-selecting leaders directing other groups, serious issues with handling translation needs, and overcrowding of groups into spaces that were too small. All of these issues were widely known among the delegates, and there was concern among many that it would be better not to use an under-resourced process no matter how much potential it may have. If you're going to promote change, do it well.

CONCLUSION

The case study of The UMC General Conference 2016 is an encouraging example of how a consensus-building approach can be crafted for, and incorporated into, any business process and polity. It provides encouragement to any church that feels constrained by strict rules of operation that it is still possible to utilize the principles and tools of a consensus-building approach.

It is clear from the experience of The UMC that one cannot assume that if you build a new model that people will flock to it. It is imperative to give attention to the realities of the context in which a church is operating, and also to be proactive, promoting, transparent, and well prepared to implement the process if people are going to trust it.

The good news from the experience of The UMC case study is that a beginning has been made, and by applying the lessons learned, the successful implementation of a new way of doing business will be possible in the future.

THE WORLD COMMUNION OF REFORMED CHURCHES AND THE USE OF DISCERNMENT PROCESSES IN DECISION-MAKING

Rev. Dr. Setri Nyomi, General Secretary of WCRC (April 2000–August 2014); Senior Pastor, Evangelical Presbyterian Church, Adenta District, Ghana.

In the period leading up to the twenty-fourth General Council held in Accra, Ghana, the then World Alliance of Reformed Churches (WARC) reviewed its decision-making processes and determined that its processes need to be aligned with the theological underpinnings of who it is and the commitment to justice that has been a hallmark of WARC. In 2002, its executive committee decided to use the consensus model of decision-making and intentionally to name it as discernment processes.

The reasons behind this decision included WARC noting that the usual parliamentary procedures were often frustrating for participants who may not understand that process. Also, when the majority of 50 percent + one votes to establish a decision, they are baffled that sometimes close to half the delegates are left unhappy. The WARC also noted that the World Council of Churches was considering these issues. The Executive Committee felt that the time had come to try something new so that more people could be included in decision-making at its General Council with integrity.

The main values that informed this direction were our need to ensure that whatever we do, especially in major decision-making, is consistent with reformed theology and ecclesiology and fosters justice for all. Christian decision-making processes need to be consistent with our faith.

Once the decision was taken, we consulted with the leadership of the Uniting Church in Australia to develop the consensus model that would fit our purposes. That process began about eighteen months before the General Council. What developed was made a part of the twenty-fourth General Council handbook. The UCA consultants mentored our team in this process and also designed an orientation program for the delegates of the General Council.

The twenty-fourth General Council in Accra became the venue for the first use of these discernment processes. It was new to most people, and therefore there were obvious challenges. The most notable of them was how the blue cards, intended to be used during discussions to express a negative take or disagreement with a point of view, or even questions, became a tool for intimidating those who were expressing those views.

This, in some cases, happened even before a person began to speak, in anticipation of his or her opinion. Those who felt they would disagree would pull out their blue cards and thrust them up so high that the speaker often felt intimidated. In some cases this also expressed a divide between the Global South and the Global North.

In evaluating we came to the conclusion that if the process was going to be used again in later WARC or WCRC processes, users need a better orientation; and WARC/WCRC needs to practice using it in its own governing body meetings and encourage churches to use it too. This is what made its use in the Uniting General Council, Grand Rapids smoother. It still had some rough edges. However, it was used in a better manner and with greater success. For Grand Rapids, the rules were also rewritten to take care of the concerns of the Executive Committee not to repeat the challenges of 2004.

For all churches and church bodies at all levels, I recommend the development processes that fit their own circumstances. The consensus model can be adapted to fit the culture and practices of any situation. My encouragement is for all to take time to study what their needs are and tailor-make a process to suit them, and acknowledge there is need for good orientation especially when it is new to so many.

In the development of consensus-model decision-making processes, churches should make use of people from churches who have significant experience in this area.

REFLECTION QUESTIONS

1. Which case study spoke most to you when you consider your context?

2. What three insights or lessons would you be sure to apply if you were introducing consensus in your organization?

ACTIVITY: SPAT EVALUATION

Use the following SPAT evaluation box as a tool to evaluate your process of making decisions in your congregation or ministry setting. Gather a leadership group to complete this activity. Write your responses in the four boxes below one at a time.

- Strengths: things you count as a blessing, a plus, a positive, or an asset as you make decisions (examples: committed leaders, clear process, adequate preparation, adequate time given to making important decisions, everyone participates, and so forth.)

- Problems: things that can distract you from or prevent good decision-making (examples: do not listen well to one another, not enough information given, lack of a behavioral guideline to guide respectful interactions, and so forth.)

- Alternatives: new ideas or different ways of making decisions that can have a significant or positive effect on your ministry (examples: start with an information session and give clear instructions, assign groups different options to research and list pros and cons of each, use smaller listening groups, and so forth.)

- Threats: things that you fear may adversely affect or harm the way your group makes decisions (examples: fear of trying something new, losing control, sharing leadership with new members, fear of growing diverse as a congregation, and so forth.)

STRENGTHS	ALTERNATIVES
PROBLEMS	THREATS

Review your SPAT carefully. Compare the responses from the various members of the group. Where do we view our process of making decisions in similar ways? Where do we have different views? (Remember that the goal of this evaluation is not to reach consensus but to reveal the various points of view that exist in the group.)

1. What things do we celebrate as our strengths?

2. Where is there need for improvement?

3. What can we change or begin to change that will make a significant, positive difference in the way we make decisions?

4. How will we manage or give attention to those things that threaten our community?

(Note: This activity can also be written to evaluate actual decisions made by the group.)

CHAPTER 8
PUTTING IT ALL TOGETHER

Building Your Discernment Process

In my younger days my youth group used to go camping to an apple or-chard that was owned by one of the church members. The camps were held in fall and winter. When I started going to camp the boys slept in an old apple packing shed. It had a concrete floor and holes in the galvanized iron walls; and we slept on blow-up mattresses that deflated while we shivered in inad-equate sleeping bags. As the week progressed people got sick, were unhappy, and had short tempers and cranky behavior. We were not happy campers!

Imagine our delight when we arrived one year and the owner had built a brand-new dormitory for the boys! It was made of wood, and the roof and walls were properly sealed against the weather. We even had bunk beds with proper mattresses. As a result of our new building, we were much more healthy and behaved much better toward one another. Yes, that new building certainly made for a better community life and much happier campers!

You are now invited to build a discernment process for your church that will be a space where people are not made sick by the experience of church meetings; where they are protected from forces that injure them and make them miserable; where the environment is such that people relate well with one another and have a positive and constructive experience.

The three elements for constructing such a place are laying a good foun-dation, putting up the walls, and then securing the roof.

DRAWING THE PLANS FOR YOUR NEW "BUILDING"

OK. You understand that if you are going to move to a consensus-building approach for decision-making then it is important to develop a plan that fits your situation. There are things that you can do that will nurture and encourage the core values and commitments of a consensus-seeking form of decision-making.

Before trying to introduce new processes into a group, it is imperative that a good foundation be laid. This foundation may be mapped out by a core leadership group or be developed by a larger group such as a board or congregation. If a smaller group does the groundwork, then it will still be necessary to get buy-in from the larger group. Buy-in will happen when people recognize that the changes that are being proposed resonate with their key values, hopes, and character.

You are reading this book and considering its ideas because you know that there is a better way for people to make decisions. You are uneasy with the status quo and yearn for a process of church decision-making that is more civil, less aggressive, collaborative, open to all views, empowering for all, fair, reasonable, more consistent with Christian values, and effective in getting things done.

The first step in developing a consensus-building decision-making approach is to talk to other people in your organization about

- what they like and dislike about the present approach to decision-making

- what they hope for when Christians meet together to make decisions

- what they think good practice for making church decisions looks like

If change is going to happen, then the conversation needs to move from an interesting idea to where the decision is made to do things differently.

There are several ways to have this conversation. As you enter into these conversations, we encourage you not to settle for tweaking or simply improving the current combative parliamentary style of decision-making in the hope that a flawed system can be salvaged. Enter into this discussion with a critical eye to the limits of the current system and offer leadership about where trans-formation can truly happen.

You might consider one or several of these approaches as a way of starting a conversation.

1. DO A CASE STUDY.

Prepare a case study based on a recent experience in your setting in which a difficult meeting took place. Have a suitably gifted person prepare the case study and analyze what contributed to the difficulties, and create a process for discussion. Some of the insights from this book may provide you with inter-pretive tools or language that help to explain what was going on. Discuss. The study should include the questions: "What happened and what could have been done better?" "What did we learn about ourselves?"

2. CONDUCT A PERFORMANCE REVIEW

Boards routinely have an annual appraisal of their performance as a leader-ship group. Judicatory bodies can undertake the same self-disciplined reflec-tion on their governance practices. Prior to the meeting that discusses the performance of the group, a survey can be sent to the membership with these and other questions:

- Over the last year, which decisions left you feeling the most satisfaction? Why?

- Over the last year, which decisions left you feeling ill at ease? Why?

- What aspects of the business processes that you use can you affirm? Why do you wish to affirm these?

- Are there areas of process that you think could be improved? Why are you concerned about these?

- What practices should a Christian body use if it is going to engage in best practice decision-making?

- What might you do differently in the future to improve your way of making decisions?

- Will you make changes? If so, what are they?

149

Have people submit their answers beforehand so that a summary sheet can be prepared for the meeting, and provide an additional resource for the discussion. Appoint a good facilitator to assist this conversation.

3. CREATE A VALUES-ALIGNMENT PROCESS

Congregations and other church bodies are concerned to ensure that their mission, ministries, and resources are aligned with their values and vision. Exercise the same discipline with respect to your business procedures.

- Does our group do church business in a way that is coherent with what we say about ourselves or how we believe Christians should behave?

- What is the goal of Christian decision-making?

- Do the methods that we use to make decisions reflect what we believe about the character of God and what we think God considers to be acceptable?

- Are the methods that we currently use theologically, culturally, and sociologically appropriate for the time and place in which we live?

- Is our way of making decisions effective in building ownership of the decisions that are made?

See chapter 4 for some examples of how a mission or values statement can be a tool for seeking alignment between what a church says about itself and how it behaves in its decision-making processes.

4. MAKE A STUDY OF GROUP DYNAMICS AND UNDERSTANDING OF PURPOSE

Participants in a group bring their own ways of working and their own objectives into a meeting. When there is significant divergence among the membership then processes can become dysfunctional and conflict can easily arise. An analysis of what people understand to be the purpose of a church meeting and its impact on how they operate in a meeting, and making these transparent for everyone to see, makes it possible to reach agreed understandings and practices.

See the examples in chapter 3 of some of the ways that people understand church meetings and how that affects the way they behave. One way into this discussion is to prepare a series of three or four questions that tease out the various views people might have about the purpose of, and practice in, meetings. Have respondents rank the strength of their response from 1 to 5. At the end of the exercise, people will score their answers so that they get a score for each of the purposes and related practices. The group now has a view on where people are coming from and can have conversations around these different perspectives and their implications for the work of the group.

5. ENGAGE IN BIBLE STUDY

See 1 Corinthians 13:4-6: "Love is patient, love is kind, it isn't jealous, it doesn't brag, it isn't arrogant, it isn't rude, it doesn't seek its own advantage, it isn't irritable, it doesn't keep a record of complaints, it isn't happy with injustice, but it is happy with the truth."

Some possible questions include the following:

- What behaviors would you expect of people in a meeting if they were showing patience and kindness and not being envious, boastful, or proud?

- In what ways would people honor one another and avoid being self-seeking, while rejoicing in the truth and not holding on to anger?

- What would it look like if your leaders were more trusting, hopeful, and persevering?

LAYING THE FOUNDATION

The foundation for the life of a Christian community is the value to which the community members ascribe. Designing a consensus-based discernment process requires identifying the foundations on which the decision-making life of the community will be built.

If values are going to shape the life of a group, then those values must result in a series of commitments that the members of the organization make to one another. Your next step in building your discernment process is to name the commitments that you will make to one another as members of a decision-making body, based on the values that you have identified and affirmed.

Throughout the book there have been examples provided of the kinds of values-based commitments or attitudes that support a consensus-based approach to discernment. You are encouraged to articulate your own commitments to one another as they arise from the values that you have affirmed.

Following is a summary of specific foundation stones that churches have found essential when using a consensus process.

OPENNESS TOWARD GOD

Participants expect to be led by the Holy Spirit and to work with God to deliver God's hopes and dreams for this community of faith. People are constantly listening for the leading of the Holy Spirit.

VULNERABILITY

People expect that they may have to change their minds. They do not come with predetermined positions or as spokespersons for others, for whom they will advocate come what may. People understand that they cannot know the will of God on their own and therefore will expect something new to develop during the course of the process.

RESPECT

Everyone is respected as an equal and valued participant in discernment. The views of all are to be heard and considered. Understand that people matter as much as, if not at times more than, the decision itself.

PATIENCE

Take the time to listen and understand what other people are saying. Take care of their well-being. Allow people to communicate in ways that are effective for them—through story, emotions, experience, and intellect.

HUMILITY

No one owns the work of discernment; it belongs to the community. Everything is offered in hope of its usefulness, without seeking to possess and control what becomes of it. People recognize the limits of their wisdom and celebrate the contributions of others.

TRUST

People are trusted to be collaborators in discernment. Trust needs to be expected, built, confirmed, and exhibited. Trusting that we are all on the same side—the side of discerning the will of God for this community in this place and time—should be the normative attitude of all participants.

TRANSPARENCY

People are honest about what they are trying to achieve, open about their motives, and clear about the processes in which they are engaged. They do not keep secrets or seek to manipulate the outcome through political maneuvering.

If these commitments reflect the values of your congregation or church body, then write them down. Produce a list of commitments that people involved in discerning the will of God can say together: "We will..." This document can be used as part of the induction process for members of governance bodies or as part of the membership orientation for new members so that they understand what they can expect from the members of your organization and what is expected of them.

If the commitments that we make to one another are the foundation stones for a discernment process, then the practices that support those commitments are the mortar that hold the bricks in place.

PUTTING UP THE WALLS

Bricks make a much better wall, building, and shelter when they are held together with mortar. Timber makes a wall when it is held together with staples and nails. People make all sorts of promises to one another about how they will behave, but when the pressure gets applied, the goodwill that people have expressed can topple over. It is naive to think that good intentions alone are enough to keep a community of people behaving well toward one another. Like bricks need mortar to make them secure, good intentions need practices to help commitments hold their shape. These walls will protect people, create a safe space for work, support healthy relationships, and strengthen the experience of community.

Once you have identified the values and commitments that you hold to as a Christian community, you need to construct the walls of your new building with practices that sustain these commitments. This is not a novel idea. We know from many areas of life that we need some disciplines and structures around us if our good intentions are going to come to life. If I am going to be healthy it is not enough just to say it; I also must do the things that support my good health. It's the same in a discernment process of the church.

There are practices that are healthy for, and sustaining of, an inclusive, respectful, civil consensus discernment, and there are some practices that actively work against such an outcome. This is the reason that we have advocated a radical rethink of how you engage in discernment, rather than just tinkering with *Robert's Rules of Order*. Most of its practices are antithetical to healthy, Christ-centered, inclusive, and respectful discernment. The practices/mortar that hold together a consensus-building form of decision-making are profoundly different. You are invited to mix up a batch of this mortar and use it to support the commitments that you have identified as important for your decision-making process. When you do so you will have good strong walls put into place with all the benefits that flow from this strength.

A. WORSHIP AND SPIRITUAL DISCIPLINES (MEANS OF GRACE)

If people are going to be obedient to God's leading, then they need to be listening for it. Prayer, worship, Holy Communion, fasting, scripture reading, contemplation, and other practices of the church sustain the believer's relationship with God and with one another. Including symbols from the Christian tradition, such as the Christ Candle, before the decision-making body helps to remind it that it is a Christian community and not just another community group. Whatever the size of the decision-making body or the length of its meeting, worship and spiritual disciplines are essential elements of church business meetings. Discernment means understanding the will of Christ for his church in a particular time and place. Discernment is impossible without openness to the Holy Spirit. The means of grace are provided in order that God's will might be revealed.

Reliance on worship and spiritual disciplines is not limited to the duration of a meeting. Before meetings a congregation, decision-making group, or wider community of faith can be called to enter into prayerful preparation for important meetings (see chapter 5).

B. BUILD COMMUNITY AND LISTEN ACTIVELY AND CAREFULLY TO EVERYONE

If people are going to work together, then they need to experience themselves as one people. Worship is the foundational element of Christian community. In addition, community is built through things as simple as being certain that people know the names of at least some of the people in the meeting, through to sharing something more deeply about themselves and what is important to them. For groups that meet with a regular membership, attention should be given to helping people reconnect after their time apart.

Ways of Building Community

- Ask the participants to share some information about themselves with others seated near them. Choose questions that are appropriate to the particular group.

- For groups that meet regularly, invite people to share what has been a positive experience since they last met and/or what has been something about which they have had a concern. Ask people to pray for one another.

- Ask people to share their hopes for this meeting and how they feel about being here.

Ways of Listening Well to One Another

Robert's Rules of Order includes a provision that a person, after a certain number of speeches, may call for the question to be put. Such a tactic to foreclose a discussion is anathema to a consensus-building approach to discernment. Establishing well-thought-out and structured ways of listening is the key to showing respect and to creating a context in which the attitudes of humility and vulnerability can be fostered. People do not have to vote to end the debate just because *Robert's Rules of Order* allow for the question to be asked!

- If people are seated around tables, they can be invited by the chairperson to talk to one another about how they feel about the business that is in front of the group. This helps the quieter people feel more comfortable to talk. People who need to process ideas through talking can start thinking out loud in a safe place. People who need to ask more questions can get help to understand from other people at the table. Persons for whom English is a second language can have more time to articulate their thoughts and gain clarity about what is happening. The views rehearsed in this setting can be shared with the larger group, or sometimes it is enough for people that they spoke in that space.

- A formal small-group process can be used where complex or contentious business needs to be addressed through a structured conversation around prepared questions. The groups respond to the proposals. Feedback goes to a drafting group, which brings a report back to a plenary session. The wisdom of the whole group is then before the plenary for further consideration.

- It is important to keep asking if anyone has a perspective that has not yet been heard.

- Allow specific cultural groups (e.g., indigenous or culturally diverse communities) to caucus together. Many times they need to develop a communal view rather than a western individualistic response. Then allow a representative of the group to bring that view back to the plenary on their behalf. This may require that the business be suspended for a time so that this can happen.

- Don't rush to a vote! Avoid the temptation to think that because it is clear that a piece of business will pass or fail that it is time to stop the discussion. Continue as long as new insights are being offered and the time allows.

- Use indicator cards. These cards allow every participant to respond quickly to each contribution or suggestion for change that is made during the deliberation phase. Traditionally orange is used to indicate warmth toward a point of view and blue to indicate that a person is cool to a suggestion or comment. Everyone can constantly express where they are up to in their thinking. Also the whole group literally sees where there is support, or not, for an idea.

- Encourage participants to engage in active listening (see chapter 2). For example, when a person responds with a story or significant emotion, the feelings can be acknowledged and the point made through a careful summary of what was being said "between the lines."

- If people are engaging constructively, allow them to speak more than once, while ensuring that a few voices do not dominate the discussion.

C. PROVIDE GOOD INFORMATION: THE INFORMATION PHASE

The first phase in a consensus-building discernment process is called the information phase. The principle is that people can only make good decisions if they know what they are doing and why. People should know everything that they need to know about the situation, the opportunity, or challenge. It is also essential that all the relevant information is before the group. Often when business comes to a meeting, only the views of the mover and seconder are given attention. However, many people in the room have a stake in the decision. The information phase therefore has to include processes that help all the people present say what is important to them, as they think about the best response to the business that is in front of them.

The Advance Documents for a Meeting

Providing good information commences with the documentation that decision-makers receive before the meeting. When business is brought before a group at the last minute, it is arguable that the group cannot be sure that it has all the information it requires. Any type of business process can insist on a date after which business will not be received for a meeting. The consideration for setting deadlines should not be how fast the photocopier can run, but whether people will have enough time to think and pray about an item of business. The deadline for receiving new business is an important part of the preparation for a business meeting and greatly assists faithful discernment. See chapter 5 for other examples of things that need to be done before the meeting actually opens, in support of a consensus-building approach.

In addition to timeliness, there are other issues that are important in the documentation. The wording of a petition or proposal needs to be clear and effective. There is nothing more confusing than words that don't make sense or, if passed, cannot be implemented. Poorly worded proposals often waste a lot of time as the meeting tries to get a clear understanding of what is intended. An alternative is to have the meeting secretary or a proposals committee rework unclear petitions and send them back to the mover and seconder with advice about how to rework them so that they make sense. New, clearer petitions will then come to the meeting. This approach is highly commended.

A similar practical or technical issue occurs when, in larger groups such as conferences, there is more than one petition that is heading in the same direction. When this happens it creates the challenge of deciding which one to address first. Also, time is spent navigating through differences in wording when the petition is something that can probably be supported by most people. In some churches there is the ability to get the movers of like-minded petitions together so they can create a new, shared petition that accommodates their positions. This strategy can significantly reduce the amount of business before a group without disrespecting the intentions of the original petitioners.

In addition to these technical strategies, significant benefits are to be derived from the way in which the rationale for a petition is presented. It is not uncommon in churches that use a parliamentary style of decision-making to see petitions that begin "wherefore this and that" and go on with saying something like "therefore be it now determined in accordance with decision XYZ..." Such legalese and dependence on being able to access the previous decisions virtually guarantee that most people will not know what is going on.

Good information requires that there is a clear rationale for the decision that is sought. Every petition should include a clear statement of the reasons for the action that is proposed. This may include a range of considerations for why this is a good thing to do, for example, theological arguments, stories, and how this action fits in with other decisions that have already been taken, if relevant. A rationale should begin a conversation about why the desired action is worthwhile and what the outcomes will be if it is supported.

Presenting the Business

Petitions should be introduced by the people who are moving and seconding them. They should provide all the facts and information necessary for people to make a well-informed decision.

Before moving to the deliberation phase, the first step is to ask whether there are questions for clarification. This is an opportunity for participants to make sure that they fully understand what is being proposed. It allows time to unpack the issues and the implications of the decision. It is hard to overstate the importance of this phase of the process! In addition to improving the chance that people know what they are doing when they use their votes, it is also very efficient, even if it takes a bit of time. How many times have you been in a meeting in which someone makes a speech and you know that person has no idea what the debate is about? Then people spend time chasing a red herring or alternatively setting that person straight. If the speaker isn't corrected, then there is the risk that people will be voting on the wrong issue! Taking time to receive questions for clarification is an indispensable part of the process and is highly valuable.

Participant Sharing

Time should be taken to understand what is at stake for the people who need to make the decision. People will be entering the discussion from the perspective of what they think is important in a discussion. It can be as small as whether the grammar is correct, through to the impact that the issue will have on a member of their family. This is important information to be shared with the group!

One of the outcomes of a consensus-building approach to decision-making is that this approach brings more people along with the decision than a simple majority will do. One can do this by paying attention to what matters to people and adjusting the words to take that into account. Such responsiveness is not about making compromises but about respecting that there are more perspectives on an issue than those brought in the first set of words that are put before the meeting. By listening to, and respecting, these perspectives, a more appropriate final resolution is possible without necessarily deflecting the original intention of the motion.

This stage of the information phase begins the movement toward the deliberation phase. By sharing what is important to them, participants have begun to indicate where they see a need for a change of words and why it matters. This step provides important information that makes it possible for others in the group to begin thinking about how they can assist one another to support the proposal. It fosters respect, concern, collaboration, and creative thinking. In some respects it is akin to classic interest-based mediation, which allows the parties to see what is important to the other and to find ways to meet those needs without necessarily having to sacrifice their interests.

D. SEEK CONSENSUS: THE DELIBERATION PHASE

Whatever the traditional practices of your organization, it is always possible to slow things down so careful consideration occurs, if there is a will to do so. In *Robert's Rules of Order* a motion can be put that the vote be taken. However, that doesn't mean the debate has to end. Even under a parliamentary process it is possible to keep listening and building consensus even after the required minimum number of speeches have been made, if the group as a whole has a will for it! This is a strong argument for the point that before making a change in your process, you build a group view that consensus-building is the healthy and faithful way to proceed. Then people will vote against the motion that the vote be put. It is critical in consensus-building not to rush to a vote but to keep listening and responding to what has been said.

One of the challenges for a group that is used to using *Robert's Rules of Order* is that there is a tendency to get caught up in amendments, substitutions, foreshadowed amendments, points of order, and other technicalities. Yet we know that this is not how we make decisions around the kitchen table! It is certainly not the way that most non-Anglo communities traditionally make community decisions. Rather, in these settings, ideas are floated and gain support, or not, and there are less formal ways to ensure that everyone understands where the discussion has reached. In the parliamentary style of decision-making, the nearest structure is for a group to meet "in committee."

There the rigid rules are suspended and things are tossed around less formally until the group reaches a point where it knows what it wants to do and ends the committee phase and moves back to formal procedures. Whatever process one traditionally uses, scope exists to implement the less formal consensus-building approach that is advocated in this book. The deliberation phase may be the greatest challenge, but it is both possible and rewarding.

Consensus-building is often a fluid process in which ideas and streams of consciousness are shared without wanting to tie down the discussion with premature documentation of motions and amendments. Moving too early to get a motion in front of the meeting forecloses the discussion by narrowing the focus too soon. So a consensus-building approach has to allow issues, experiences, ideas, stories, and other theological considerations into the room before trying to document the developing direction.

Later in this chapter there will be more specific guidance offered on how to manage the consensus-building process. Here are some key elements to consider:

- The process commences with the speakers offering themes, considerations, and suggestions.

- Using indicator cards allows the chair and the membership of the meeting to see if there is support for each view as it is offered.

- It is not necessary to react to every set of orange or blue cards. The discussion can proceed until a direction is identified. Since most motions have several elements, it is helpful if the chairperson identifies that there has not been discussion on several sections and tests whether that means that they are acceptable. If they are acceptable, they can be put aside as accepted until the final decision time.

- Eventually the chairperson focuses the discussion on a section of the proposal and views that are expressed. An alert chairperson, supported by a good meeting secretary and note taker, can suggest that there is a direction developing that seems to have significant support and then offer wording that captures the discussion up to that point.

A powerful and effective option in the deliberation phase is the use of a formal small-group process. This is where people meet in pre-arranged groups with designated leaders to work through a consultative process and finally report to the facilitation group on their deliberations. The facilitation group then reports back to the plenary session on the outcome of those discussions.

Through these processes concerns are raised, collaborative solutions are found, points of continuing disagreement are identified, and a final form of words is crafted to be tested. This process can proceed within nearly any business process until the point where it is time to determine the mind of the meeting. After the listening, generating and testing of alternatives, and caring for one another, the time is reached where a decision needs to be recorded.

E. SUBMISSION TO THE WISDOM OF THE GROUP: THE DETERMINATION PHASE

Making the Decision

Discernment as a community of faith requires that a point is reached when the deliberation ends and a decision is made. A decision does not need to be only for or against the original wording. A decision may be that more information is required before a decision can be made or that further processes (e.g., study or prayer) need to take place before it is time to act, or that an alternative way to tackle an issue has been identified and a time to think and pray about it is appropriate before deciding what to do (i.e., the decision is deferred to a later meeting). A consensus-building approach to discernment does not get hooked into whether the decision is for or against the original words. This process is interested in what is our best, faithful assessment of the step that we should take next.

The strategies and resources presented here are offered on the premise that they can be used in a wide variety of polities and business procedures. Therefore, it is appropriate to acknowledge that in many situations it will be necessary to move "out of committee" and into the formal or legally required business procedures of the body. Whether this process reverts to *Robert's Rules of Order* or to a bishop having the final vote, the possibility remains that the final version of words that is being resolved has been developed using a consensus-building approach. If that phase has been done well, then a final formal vote will be supported by far more than 50 percent of the people. Consensus will have been built.

Assuming that the context in which you operate is not able to make decisions through the consensus of the whole group, there is one more step that can be considered before returning to the formal decision-making method that is used in your context.

There are churches that seek to make their decisions by consensus. Consensus does not mean unanimity. It means unity even if there is not 100 percent agreement with a decision because those who still disagree are willing to step aside and accept the wisdom of the group.

The Uniting Church in Australia provides an example of such a church. Many times it will reach a point in a meeting during which nearly everyone agrees on the course of action that should be taken, but still some people cannot agree. At this point the persons in the minority can hopefully live out of the theological heart of this approach, which is that it is the community that needs to be respected as the way in which discernment happens. At this point, the minority is asked whether they consider that their views have been heard and if they are willing to stand aside so that consensus can be recorded. In the Uniting Church in Australia, it is possible for people in this situation to affirm that they have been heard and that they are willing to stand aside in order that the meeting may move to a decision.

PUTTING ON THE ROOF

The foundations have been laid, the bricks are held together, and the walls have been erected. This new meeting space is taking shape. All it requires now is a roof to protect the people inside from the elements.

CREATING SAFE SPACES

Supporting the whole process is an environment in which people feel safe to participate. If this is missing, then people will not enter into the other practices that allow healthy and respectful discernment processes to operate.

Meeting procedures need to be aware of, and address, power imbalances. Power imbalances can be based on gender, race, ethnicity, age, language, ordination, institutional power, capacity to manage well in the prevailing business procedures, and many other factors.

Every member has a personal responsibility to show respect and to try to empower the other members of the community to make their contribution. However, structures and disciplines need to be in place so that best practice is seen as normative and supported. Various strategies are available to embed healthy practices. For example:

- liturgically reinforcing covenants about how people will behave in a meeting

- training in cross-cultural and gender sensitivity

- having complaints procedures for where people have been subject to inappropriate behavior

- providing opportunities for people who have found the presuppositions and practices of the dominant culture oppressive to share their experience

PROPERLY TRAINED LEADERSHIP

Leaders who are well chosen, trained, and supported are essential to the effectiveness of any meeting process. The skills required for a consensus-building process, and the resources that are required, are significantly different to those used in a parliamentary style of decision-making. Failure to attend to the recruitment, support, and training of leaders is like setting up a new home and leaving the roof off. You can guarantee that it will not be a pleasant place to be!

EVALUATING THE EXPERIENCE

It is our hope that the principles and practices that are presented in this book will become part of the natural pattern of church life. When you try something new, it is important to take some time to evaluate the experience. It is always possible to improve processes, so make sure that when you undertake a new process that you have a good evaluation plan. This allows you to continue to learn and improve your process and gives people confidence that you are respecting them as they move into this new space.

SUMMARY

Designing a consensus process takes thought and time. It is tempting to grab hold of a few techniques and insert them into a new setting. However, this approach will fail because the new processes and practices are not understood and valued by the people who are using them. In that situation the techniques end up feeling like a fad and support for using them fades very quickly.

The good news is that you can design and build a consensus-building process that is appropriate for your setting. The steps are clear and, when followed, will work for you and your organization:

- Lay your foundation. Identify the values of your organization.

- Gather up the building blocks and secure them together. These are commitments you make to one another.

- Erect the walls. They are the practices that support your commitments.

- Set the roof. These are safe places, training, and evaluation.

When you follow these steps and develop ownership of them across your group, then you have designed and built a place where you will be best able to discern the will of God for your community.

SOME TECHNIQUES AND TOOLS USED IN A CONSENSUS-BUILDING PROCESS

As noted in chapter 5 there are four phases in implementing a process of decision making that is healthy, inclusive, and effective: preparation, invitation, deliberation and decision, and implementation. Chapter 5 includes examples of processes and practices that can be used in these various parts of the cycle of discernment.

This section offers some very specific examples of what can be done to support discernment in a meeting. It is not possible to offer a script for every possible contingency that might arise. This is why in your planning for a meeting it is important to think about how you will manage the flow of business and develop your own strategies to effectively do this. Nevertheless, it is possible to learn from the experience of others so here are some ideas. The resources will be presented under the headings for the four steps that constitute a consensus-building approach: Gathering the Community, Information, Deliberation, and Determination.

1. GATHERING THE COMMUNITY

Take your time and do this well. Some of these steps can be commenced before the meeting starts.

Welcome

Small groups and church boards may not consider this step to be important since it is assumed that everyone knows and feels comfortable with one another. However, people come to meetings in all kinds of moods and with different things on their minds. Helping people in reconnecting with one another and having their concerns acknowledged is an important way to be a welcoming community.

The setting and layout of the meeting space and the elements of hospitality that are offered are also important ways to welcome people as they gather as a community.

When larger groups meet it is very important to think about the way that people are gathered into this community. It is quite common for participants to sit in predesignated seats according to the area from which they come. This custom restricts the connection with the other participants and should be resisted where possible. People are in a community of the whole body and not just hanging around with the people that they know well.

Larger groups should give special attention to activities that act as ice breakers and allow people to start connecting with one another at a deeper level. Examples of such community-building questions that can be discussed in table groups or with the person next to them are where they have come from, how they spend most of their time, and what they hope for from the meeting.

Groups that meet over several days should give serious consideration to a social opportunity early in their meeting time. It may be as simple as a supper after the opening worship or a shared lunch. But it allows members to meet one another as fellow disciples and not as debating partners.

Worship

The group size and length of the meeting will influence the rituals and liturgical acts that can be employed. Larger gatherings, or the first meeting of a new church board, could include Holy Communion. Other activities include identifying hopes and concerns in a liturgical setting and praying for one another, being encouraged by scripture and sermons, passing the peace and lighting a Christ Candle. All have their part to play in connecting people with God and one another in the common cause of faithful discernment.

Set Guidelines for Participation

Many groups have documents that express their expectations of the participants. Areas covered by such documents include cross-cultural sensitivity, policies on sexual harassment, anti-triangulation, bullying, and intimidation; ways of working together that emphasize collaboration and not competition; and clearly documented complaint procedures into which participants are inducted for use when these policies are breached.

These policies and procedures need to be presented regularly to the group, and commitment to adhere to them sought. Liturgical expressions of these commitments can work very well.

Make sure that everyone knows the rules under which the meeting will operate. If you develop new rules or have new people joining your group, make sure that you allocate time to make it clear how the meeting rules work. For groups that meet often it can be part of the annual induction process. For annual meetings it can be time that is set aside early in the meeting. Whether you are using familiar meeting rules or new ones, don't assume that people understand them. Gathering a community is about ensuring that everyone is in a position to participate. If they don't know the rules, they cannot effectively function.

Agree on the Agenda

Agreeing to the agenda can often seem unnecessary. However, if the meeting belongs to the whole group, then members should participate in establishing its program. One of the opportunities around adopting the agenda in a consensus-building process is that it allows a space to let people know why certain things are being done in a certain order. For example, if a formal small-group process is used, it is always wise to point out that the introduction of the issue will happen at point A, the small groups will happen at point B, and then the report of the facilitation group will be brought at point C. This gives people confidence that they know what is happening and when they will have the best opportunity to participate.

2. INFORMATION

Introduction

The topic or proposal is presented. The information session may be a report with recommendations, a proposal with a rationale, or a presentation on a topic of importance to the group without any preconceived ideas about where the discussion will lead.

Whatever format the introduction takes the goal is to increase the understanding of the members on what the issue is, why it is important, and what might be done in response to this issue.

Where there are recommendations for action, the persons moving and seconding the proposal are at liberty to speak and make their case for the proposed course of action. In doing so they should, in their preparation, have been strongly encouraged to focus on the values and objectives that they want to achieve and not just the words of the petition. Many motions are detailed and concentrate on strategy, whereas there are often many ways to achieve a goal. So encouraging dialogue at the level of goals and values helps to open up the options when it comes to the specific strategies or actions that are taken.

Questions for Clarification

Receive, and respond to, as many questions for clarification as necessary to be sure that people understand the issues that are before them. The persons responding to the questions will probably be the mover or seconder, but there may be questions of a financial, legal, or other specialist nature to which another person is better placed to answer. This is not a time to debate the merits, so the chairperson needs to be willing to call comments out of order, or if someone looks to be making a speech to press the speaker to come to a question.

Ways to Draw Out the Questions

Asking questions at the microphone in a plenary session or around the table with a small group is one way of identifying the questions that people have. However, there are other options:

- When the business is known ahead of time, members could submit questions for clarification to the mover and seconder before the meeting. Answers could be provided after the presentation of the issue either verbally or in writing.

- If people are seated at round tables or in small groups, the questions can be surfaced in that setting in the first instance. The chairperson can say, "In your table groups share with one another what questions come to your mind as you think about this petition." Or, "What more do you need to know before you can discuss this petition?"

- For particularly complex subjects it might be possible to stop the process at the end of the first round of questions for clarification and come back to it at a later session. During that time other questions may have surfaced or answers sought from the presenters.

Types of Information That Should Be Sought

A bridge conversation between the questions for clarification and the deliberation phase is to invite people to share their concerns and hopes as they hear the petition presented. This is an invitation to share another important piece of information: what is at stake in the issue. Sometimes people don't see the whole impact of what they are proposing. As directions are sought for action, it will be important for a person to know information and what the impact of a certain decision will be.

Invitational questions from the chairperson might include the following:

- When you heard the presentation, did you think that any issue was overlooked?
- When you come to discuss this petition, what is going to be important for you?
- What is at stake for you in this issue?

Once again the questions can be answered first in smaller groups or directly in the plenary.

At the appropriate point, the chairperson needs to confirm that all the questions have been asked and to indicate that the deliberation phase will commence. Often this juncture will become clear as more people find themselves talking about concerns or support rather than questions for clarification.

Chairpersons should be alert to whether opening up the issue has given rise to feelings that require a pastoral or worshipful response. A rhythm of prayer and worship is a natural part of a consensus-building approach and should be drawn upon whenever it is helpful to do so.

3. DELIBERATION

The size of the group, the familiarity of the members with one another, and the frequency of their meeting will impact the way in which they conduct their meetings. Some of the techniques that are used in consensus-building churches may not be necessary for a local church board or a small congregation—for example, the use of colored cards or the formal small-group and facilitation-group process. However, even if these tools are not used, the principles are still to be applied, that is, ensuring that everyone has an opportunity to be heard, that the minority voices get a good hearing, and that new ideas are given a chance to get worked into the final decision.

In smaller meetings it is the responsibility of the chairperson and secretary to ensure that people have the opportunity to participate and that the ideas that come up are appropriately considered. This can be achieved by use of questions or, better still, by creating a culture and practice of inclusion and respect.

The techniques and tools that are offered below are able to work in formal and less-formal settings and in small and large groups. However, the level of complexity will be increased the larger the group, the more complex the business before the meeting, and how contentious it is. As you consider the following processes, remember that not every piece of business is complicated! Some acts of discernment can be achieved relatively quickly without much time spent in some of these phases. That is fine as long as the principles of empowering every voice, listening to the minority, and seeking to build consensus are still applied.

Using Indicator Cards

Indicator cards are used so that every member of the group has an opportunity to participate throughout the discussion. Orange cards are used to indicate warmth or support toward a point that has been made. Blue reflects that a person is cool to an idea. Blue cards can also be used to indicate that a person is not ready to make a decision, either because he or she needs more information or cannot yet agree.

Cards are displayed at the end of each contribution. They are shown by holding them at shoulder height and are not waved around in an aggressive manner. When they are used as a way of expressing an opinion, it is not necessary to clap, cheer, or jeer at speakers. Indeed a consensus-building approach would never support such practices as they perpetuate division and hinder the involvement of some people.

Using indicator cards keeps people engaged because, depending on the responses that are made, the direction of the meeting can change. In a consensus-building approach it is not possible to switch off from the deliberation until it is time to vote, as new ideas are constantly arising and can change the discussion.

Indicator cards are a helpful method for empowering every voice in the room, since it is easier to hold a card than to speak at a microphone. When people show their cards, it is easy for the whole meeting to see where the thinking of the group is on a particular point. This assumes that people don't hold their cards back to back and give one signal to the people in front of them and another to those behind! This technique is a powerful one for allowing the silent majority a voice. In this process it is not the eloquence of the speaker that indicates the mind of the meeting but the members as they respond to each point made.

Simple questions by the chairperson such as "How are you feeling about that suggestion?" or comments such as "It would be helpful if you can indicate your response to each presentation" encourage use of indicator cards until their use becomes natural.

A Formal Small-Group Process

Usually this process is used in larger meetings that run for more than one day. However, the model can be used in a congregational setting in which the discussion is then deferred until the report of the facilitation group can come back to the next meeting of the congregation. The appendix has examples of the documentation that can be used in this process.

This process has the following elements:

- Information session: The issue is introduced in a plenary session, and questions for clarification are received and responded to in the plenary session.

- Small groups: These groups are preselected to ensure that they reflect the diversity of the meeting. There are twelve to fifteen people in each group including a leader. Leaders have received training and resources that support their work. The small groups go through the process of deliberation on the proposal, sharing their issues and concerns as well as possible alternatives. They record their position on the original proposal on a prepared reporting form and also document proposed amendments and their level of support, and write up the issues that have arisen in the group, even if they are not a majority view. The report of the group discussion is then handed to the facilitation group.

- Facilitation group: This group reviews the feedback and identifies the level of support for the original petition and the new ideas and issues that have been raised. It prepares a report on what has arisen in the small groups. The report includes information on levels of support for the original wording and amendments and where new ideas and considerations are documented. The facilitation group presents a revised motion based on the input from the small groups and its sense of how to address the issues that have been raised.

- Plenary session: The report is presented and is open to questions and then is received. The revised proposal becomes the basis for the next stage of the deliberation phase, and consensus-building can continue.

If this process is used, then it is important to ensure that there is sufficient time between the end of the small-group session and the time by which the facilitation group needs to report to a plenary session.

Building Consensus

An important feature of consensus-building is that people can change their minds. So it is important to allow the conversation to flow for a time before rushing to a decision or to major amendments. As people begin to speak they should be encouraged to talk about the values and principles that inform their thinking. Issues should be raised without rushing to judgment about the way to respond to those issues. People can recognize many issues as important, and not only those that were in the minds of the original mover and seconder.

The use of indicator cards makes it possible to recognize the things that are important for the group. As the discussion continues there will be suggestions made that address the issues that have been identified. One suggestion may be to add new elements to the motion. Perhaps there will be a growing view that the action proposed is not the right one for this time, and another course of action is more helpful. There may be changes of wording offered that address the difficulties faced by some members of the meeting. As each of these offerings are made, the meeting indicates its level of support. Some useful comments and questions at these points include the following:

- This new idea seems to have quite a bit of support. Do we want to incorporate it into the motion for the purpose of our discussion?

- We are not making a decision on this now; we are just testing the level of support for this idea.

173

- This idea has some support; let's spend a bit of time focusing on this section of the motion for a while and see where it goes.

- It doesn't look like that idea is going to fly. If people want to advance it again, or a variation of it, then they can do so; but it looks at the moment as though the group doesn't want to go in that direction.

- There seems to be a mixed view around these ideas, and we are not moving forward at present. Take some time in your table group to discuss resolving this impasse, and we will return to the discussion with the ideas you come up with.

- Does anyone have a suggestion on how this motion can be changed to make it possible for more people to support it?

Listening to All the Voices

Use of indicator cards, discussions around table groups, and the formal small-group process are powerful ways of giving voice to the often silent members of a meeting. More important than techniques are the values of the group. People need to experience respect, deep listening, concern for them as people, and encouragement to participate. No technique will ensure that all people are heard. However, when people know that their views are important and appreciated because of the way that the group behaves, then there are techniques that enhance the breadth of participation.

Some cultural groups do not come to a position as individuals the way that western society values. Some cultures have a hierarchy of who may contribute and in what way. Therefore, communal reflection on a topic may be necessary for some of these groups before the views of a particular community can be heard. On such occasions communities may need to take time out of the meeting to discuss an idea, rather than letting individuals presume that they can speak for their community. On their return, the appropriate representative of the group can be asked to present the thinking of the group.

Invite the people showing blue cards to offer their points of view. Do not rush to a decision. Following are examples of invitational questions:

- Does anyone showing a blue card want to speak?

- Do you have anything to offer that you think the group has not yet heard?

- Do you think that the group has considered your point of view?

- Is there any change that can be made to the motion that will make it possible for you to support it?

Getting to the Words That Express Consensus

As the deliberation phase continues there will be a growing sense of where there is support. Some of this consensus will have been documented as the discussion unfolded. One of the benefits of a consensus-building approach is that it does not rely on formal amendments, substitutions, and notices of amendments. Instead opportunities to build agreement are taken as and when they arise.

It is important that the chairperson keeps people well informed about the changes to the motion that are being considered. Keeping people informed is achieved by giving clear explanations, seeking feedback, taking a straw vote to include something in the motion, and so on. The important thing is that when such changes are made they are documented and clearly presented to the meeting. The most effective way to do this is to have the wording on a screen or newsprint, so that the original words and the alternative can be seen, and when a change is agreed it is then incorporated into the wording that becomes the basis for ongoing discussion. It should be emphasized that a decision has not yet been taken. What is happening here is documenting a view on what most people think the decision should include. It is building a consensus on what words are required in order to make it possible for people to support the motion.

This highly responsive and flexible approach works most easily for simple issues and in smaller groups. When groups are used to the process it is possible to employ it on increasingly complex matters. Drafting words on the floor of a meeting is always a challenge, but a good meeting secretary can often capture the sentiments that have been expressed by various speakers and offer words back to the group. There will also be gifted people in the body of the meeting who can offer this service.

In situations where things get stuck, there are a number of options.

175

If people are seated at round tables, they can be asked to identify words that will provide a breakthrough. This often works because it makes it possible to get a clearer handle on the issues that are behind the blockage and the words can then follow.

If possible, defer further discussion on this issue to a later session. It is amazing what a break can do for energy levels and insight!

Send the representatives of the views who seem to be struggling to reach agreement out of the room and ask them to work toward an agreement and return to offer a way through.

Breaks can be taken for prayer, silence, music, pastoral responses, and other interventions that support people through the process.

Identify through straw votes where there is already a high level of agreement and where more work is required. Focus the discussion on the latter.

4. DETERMINATION

Each type of church meeting will have its own way of making a decision. At the appropriate time in the process the meeting will move from the deliberation phase to the determination or decision-making phase.

When the group moves to that point it will be important for everyone to be clear on the decision that they are being asked to make. The final words of the motion need to be clear.

If the consensus-building approach has gone well, then this phase should be relatively short since there will already be significant numbers in agreement with the final words. If it is seen as helpful, a vote can be taken on the motion in its parts.

If there is a significant minority still opposed to the motion, the question could be asked whether a decision has to be taken at this time. If the issue does not have to be resolved at this meeting, then the decision could be deferred and further work done so that a greater number of people can support the decision.

Irrespective of the way a decision is actually taken, it is acceptable to check in with the people who are not yet on board to see whether they can accept it and to revisit the question of whether a decision is really required at this time. This can be very important where there is a significant minority who opposes the motion.

CONCLUSION

The consensus-building approach advocated for in this book can be used with any polity or size meeting. Whether the decision is ultimately taken by a vote consensus can be reached.

Groups that use consensus in their meetings are more cohesive, cooperative, and respectful and more reflective of the character of Christ.

We realize that this process may seem complex and cumbersome, but we assure you that the more you try, the easier it becomes to use. Be bold and begin!

THE PRAYER OF ARCHBISHOP OSCAR ROMERO

It helps, now and then, to step back and take a long view.
The kingdom is not only beyond our efforts; it is even beyond our vision.
We accomplish in our lifetime only a tiny fraction of the magnificent enterprise that is God's work.

Nothing we do is complete, which is a way of saying that the
Kingdom always lies beyond us.
No statement says all that could be said. No prayer fully expresses our faith.

No confession brings perfection.
No pastoral visit brings wholeness.
No program accomplishes the Church's mission. No set of goals and objectives includes everything.
This is what we are about.

We plant the seeds that one day will grow.
We water seeds already planted,
knowing that they hold future promise.
We lay foundations that will need further development.
We provide yeast that produces effects far beyond our capabilities.
We cannot do everything, and there is a sense of liberation in realizing that.

This enables us to do something and to do it very well.
It may be incomplete, but it is a beginning, a step along the way,

177

an opportunity for the Lord's grace to enter and do the rest. We may never see the end results, but that is the difference between the master builder and the worker.

We are workers, not master builders; ministers, not messiahs.

We are prophets of a future not our own. Amen.[1]

---

1. Bishop Kenneth Untener's Prayer. Used by Permission of Little Books of the Diocese of Saginaw, Michigan.

AFTERWORD

This book is a labor of love. We genuinely love the people of the church and the Christ who has called them into a new community as the people of God. We also love the people the church is called to serve.

We are concerned that

- people are leaving the church over decisions poorly made
- many people from culturally diverse communities, women, and young people find *Robert's Rules of Order* so at odds with their normal way of making decisions that they are excluded from our decision-making processes
- many millennials refuse to participate in *Robert's Rules of Order*
- people know us more for our fights than our love
- congregations are diverted from their mission because of unresolved conflict and divisions caused through poor meeting processes
- pastors, district superintendents, and bishops are expending significant amounts of time, money, and emotional energy in addressing splits in churches that would have never happened if only decisions were made using a consensus-based approach

As we have looked at the pain that has been caused to these people by the way that decisions have been made in the church, our hearts grieve. Jesus grieves. So much hurt. So much distraction from the mission of the church. So many people estranged from God and the church because Christians have been unable to make decisions in ways that are aligned with Christian character and practices.

In writing this book, our hope is that Christian fellowship and mission will be enhanced. We believe that when the church moves to a consensus-building approach to decision-making, there will be less pain, less financial loss, and less diversion of resources and effort, and more faithful decisions than happens under *Robert's Rules of Order.*

When you finish this book, we want you to be empowered to support the implementation of our discernment process that is aligned with Christian values and is contextually relevant. We believe that this process will help you make better decisions. We want you to provide a more faithful Christian witness in the world. This book is a practical guide, and its value lies in using its insights and practical strategies. We want you to finish this book with hope, with increased capacity to support and bring about change, and with the tools that will help build a healthy way for your church to be in community around contentious issues.

Share with us what you have learned, your questions, and your experiences as you undertake the transformation that will positively impact the quality of your church life and its mission. We'd love to hear from you. Join our community of encouragement and learning at making churchdecisions.com and commenting on the blog posts; following us on Facebook @makingchurchdecisions; or send an e-mail to julia@making churchdecisions.com or terence@makingchurchdecisions.com.

We will continue our work and support for a consensus-building approach to decision-making throughout the church. This is an ongoing conversation. We will be available to

- lead training events such as seminars and workshops
- coach pastors and board chairs
- provide keynote presentations
- facilitate large meetings such as annual conferences and religious boards of directors
- link with transformative leaders for mutual encouragement and learning as they change the way their church makes decisions

We look forward to the continuing conversation.

In conclusion, we want to express our sincere gratitude to friends and colleagues from around the world, who contributed to this work and have helped to make this book a much richer and more helpful resource. Special thanks to our family and friends who have supported and encouraged us as we have undertaken this major project. May our grandchildren grow as disciples of Christ in a church that proclaims the good news for all and lives true to the character of the body of Christ. We also owe a special debt of gratitude to Paul Franklyn and David Teel from the editorial team at Abingdon Press, without whose confidence, guidance, and expertise this book would not have been possible.

Thanks be to God, the Creating Father, Redeeming Son, and Sustaining Holy Spirit. May all glory be given to God in the church now and forever.

DISCERNMENT CHECKLIST

Each of the following blocks contains a part of the discernment process. Together, they form a process of making decisions by consensus. Review this material and use it as a checklist as you move through your process.

Phase 1: Preparation

Name the issue(s), think about meeting preparation including who will fill key roles, seek prayer support, and set meeting guidelines.

Review this material on pages 86–92.

- ❏ Decide the issue to come before the group
- ❏ Decide goal(s) of the process: what do you want to accomplish?
- ❏ Form a process planning group
- ❏ Develop a master plan for your process
- ❏ Make a budget for facilitator, supplies, and so on
- ❏ List people who will be affected by the decision
- ❏ Design a communication strategy
- ❏ Plan means of grace to support the process (Bible study, prayer, and so on)
- ❏ If you do not have one, complete a behavioral covenant
- ❏ Review the information phase
  - ❏ Identify the information required by participants
  - ❏ Plan for information distribution (make copies and so on)
- ❏ Review the deliberation phase
  - ❏ Decide who will prepare the proposal
  - ❏ Decide on a facilitator
  - ❏ Decide if you will use small groups. If so,
    - ❏ Recruit the facilitation team (five to seven people)
    - ❏ Assign participants to small groups
    - ❏ Recruit small-group leaders
    - ❏ Recruit small-group recorders
    - ❏ Choose spaces for the groups to meet
    - ❏ Provide training

Phase 2: Invitation
Let people know what the issues will be, and invite their prayers and presence.
Prime the process so people are not hitting the issue cold.

Review this material on pages 92–93.

❏ Decide who needs to be at the meeting and make a list
❏ Communicate with your congregation or organization
    ❏ Write and send an open letter
    ❏ Make announcements
    ❏ Make a presentation
    ❏ Post on your website
❏ Introduce the process leaders to the congregation and bless them (facilitator, small-group leaders, and so on)
❏ Call for a season of prayer

Phase 3: Decision Point
Decide which items of business will best be addressed through the various tools that are used as part of a consensus-building approach to discernment and plan the meeting accordingly.

Review this material on pages 93–95.

- ❏ Gather the Community
    - ❏ Welcome
    - ❏ Worship or devotion
    - ❏ Review guidelines for participation
    - ❏ Adopt the agenda
    - ❏ Provide an overview of the process

- ❏ Information Phase
    - ❏ Present the topic to be discussed
    - ❏ Share related information
    - ❏ Respond to questions for clarification
    - ❏ Allow time for people to share what is important to them as they consider the issue
- ❏ Deliberation Phase
    - ❏ Choose method to consider the proposal and discern options
        - ❏ Small groups, pairs, or trios
            - ❏ Consider the proposal
            - ❏ Complete response worksheet
    - ❏ Collect the worksheets or gather responses

- ❏ Determination Phase
    - ❏ Look at revised proposal or petition
    - ❏ Make the decision in an appropriate way (vote, ballot, and so on)

Phase 4: Implementation
Document who will take responsibility for the implementation of the decision, decide timelines for action, and evaluate the process. Celebrate concluding the process.

Review this material on pages 95–96.

❏   Share the decision with the congregation or organization and affirm why it is right for the group
    ❏   Letter
    ❏   Newsletter article
    ❏   Presentation
    ❏   Website
    ❏   E-mail

❏   Thank people for their participation and support

❏   Respond to the concerns and hopes of the community

❏   Assess the process

When you finish your decision-making process, evaluate your steps by asking:
    1.   What steps did you do well?
    2.   What steps need improvement?
    3.   What changes would you make next time?

LEADERSHIP ROLE DESCRIPTIONS

FACILITATOR'S ROLE

1. DESIGN THE PROCESS

There are many tools and techniques that can be employed in delivering an effective consensus process. An expert facilitator works with the group preparing the meeting to put in place the elements that meet their particular needs. By looking at the agenda and the different business that will be before the meeting, it is possible to plan in advance which of these tools are best suited for particular business.

When there is business that is complex or contentious or of major significance to the organization, it will be appropriate to use the small groups and facilitation group. In this situation careful consideration needs to be given to the order of the agenda and the timing of the various parts of the process.

A facilitator will be aware of the four steps of the discernment cycle that need to be present in order to undertake an effective discernment process. The design will take these steps into account and reflect the unique context of each organization.

2. MENTOR AND GUIDE

When groups enter into a new way of doing things, there is much that seems strange and uncertain. There is a natural tendency to fall back into familiar patterns. A facilitator who knows the path provides encouragement, guidance, and mentoring to the leadership group. The facilitator can be important in holding a group accountable to see through the implementation of a new process by stressing the importance of steps that may not be as obvious to people who are new to a consensus-building approach.

3. PRODUCE THE DOCUMENTATION

Within organizations there are different ranges and depths of expertise. A facilitator will bring broad expertise in the area of producing resources and documentation to the team. At the very least this will include training materials, small-group process sheets in support of the small group leaders, and reporting sheets for submission to the facilitation group.

The facilitator should also document the plan that has been designed in step one, which clearly lays out the tasks, timelines, and responsible persons for the key elements of the process.

Some facilitators may also be used to produce invitation letters for prospective leaders, key messages that can be part of the communication plan, YouTube pieces, and other communication support.

4. TRAIN AND SUPPORT PERSONS LEADING THE PROCESS

Before the meeting, and on site, provide training and support for the chair of the meeting, the meeting secretary, the facilitation group and its convenor, and the small-group leaders.

5. PROVIDE A REPORT

Deliver an independent assessment of how the process operated, emphasizing its strengths and outcomes and noting where there is potential to improve.

RESPONSIBILITIES OF THE SMALL-GROUP LEADER

The role of the small group leader is to

- facilitate a discussion that will allow all the members of the group to express their feelings, views, and opinions about the proposal that is before them

- empower the members of the group to generate amendments to the proposals that have the highest level of support among the group's members

- record the strength of support, or otherwise, for the original proposal (in whole or in part) and do the same for any amendments that are developed, using the document that has been prepared for this purpose

- check with the group that the record matches the mind of the group

- ensure that the facilitation group receives the group report at the agreed time

QUALITIES OF THE SMALL-GROUP LEADER

Experienced small-group leaders might come from various backgrounds. Examples are educators and experienced small-group leaders who use a nondirective approach, mediators from a facilitative school of practice, counselors, and so on. They have the following attributes:

- capacity to be a servant of the organization that is meeting and the process

- ability to put aside personal views in order to facilitate the group

- spiritual, emotional, and psychological capacity to be nondirective

While recognizing that everyone has a view on any proposal, a small-group leader is someone who is trusted not to seek to impose their will on the group.

RESPONSIBILITIES OF THE FACILITATION GROUP

The role of the facilitation group is to

- receive the reports from the small groups
- prayerfully and carefully identify trends and directions that arise from the reports
- seek to hear the "voice" of the members of the meeting as expressed through the feedback from the small groups
- develop a report that is used to advise the members of the meeting about the views that have been expressed from across all the groups about the proposals that went into the process, with particular reference to where there is support, limited support, or no clear direction emerging and why this seems to be so
- present new ideas and possible directions that have been identified by the participants through the small-group process
- bring a report to a plenary session of the meeting

The next phase of the deliberation will happen through the report. Proposals that the facilitation group believes give voice to the "mind of the meeting" and/or provide options for a way forward will be used to lead this discussion. This will be based on what the small-group reports are saying is the reason for a lack of agreement, even though the words may not have been offered by a majority of groups.

The convenor must ensure that the report is delivered to the relevant officers by the expected time.

The facilitation group leader presents the report of the facilitation group to a plenary session of the meeting, and responds to questions of the report.

QUALITIES OF THE MEMBERS OF THE FACILITATION GROUP

While recognizing that everyone has a view on the proposals, facilitation group members are trusted not to seek to impose their will on the meeting through this process. They will have wide acceptance as being able to serve the whole group (i.e., not rigid or partisan).

People of great spiritual integrity and sensitivity with a capacity to offer servant leadership are critical to the process.

Within the facilitation group as a whole there needs to be the following attributes:

- spiritual gifts and graces that fit people to engage in a process of discernment
- capacity to identify trends from a myriad of detail
- ability to work carefully with a lot of detailed information but not get lost in it
- skills in summarizing and reframing (in the counselor and mediator sense of those skills)
- ability to work in a team setting with a tight timeline
- skills in drafting legislation

People who are educators, counselors, mediators, and skilled people in drafting petitions are often helpful in this role.

FACILITATION GROUP CONVENER ROLE

The convener leads a team of five to seven people who have the responsibility of assisting the meeting to hear its voice through the work that has been done in the small-group process.

Before the meeting, take the following steps:

- Know the proposals that will be going into the process and the documentation that will be used in the small groups, especially the reporting sheet.
- Make contact with the other facilitation group members and begin to build a sense of team. Also get to know them and their strengths.
- Liaise with the facilitator, if there is one, and receive coaching.

- Think about what methodology will be used to analyze the many reports that will be received. For example: Will all of them be read to the whole group, or will it be done in sub-groups? Will you use a grid on a whiteboard to capture the input? How will you "hold" the various suggestions that come through the reporting sheets?

- Make sure that a comfortable meeting place has been arranged for the group, with access outside of normal business hours. Ensure that you have all the materials you need including coffee and food, if you are working over mealtimes.

- Know where the small-group response sheets will be delivered.

Work with the feedback in the following ways:

- Collect the small-group response sheets.

- Welcome the team and do introductions. If the team members do not know one another, do a simple team-building exercise.

- Suggest a way of processing the reports; take feedback and have the team agree on the method that will work best for them.

- Work through the process, being mindful of when breaks are needed and other ways to support the group.

- Be prepared to remind team members if they seem to be bringing their own agenda to the group and call them back to their servant role.

- Ensure that the draft report is prepared, reviewed by the team, and delivered to the relevant support staff in time for printing and distributing at the plenary session (although the report is not always printed).

Present the report:

- Present the report to the plenary session.

- Answer questions on the report.

- If you are a member of the meeting, move the reception of the report.

SAMPLE PROCESS AGENDA

SMALL GROUP #1 - DATE, TIME

The first session should spend time building community, setting expectations, and orienting people to the process. Subsequent sessions will have a much shorter gathering component, say fifteen minutes.

These resources are designed to assist your working group meetings. You are welcome to draw on your own experience and resources to help the group develop a sense of community and to work well together.

GATHERING

Ensure that people are seated in a circle and are able to make eye contact with one another.

1. Welcome

Introduce yourself and invite people to say their name and where they are from; or do another appropriate activity if people already know something about one another.

2. Opening Prayer

3. Community-Building

Invite people to talk in pairs. Explain that they will each briefly introduce their partner to the group following their conversation. (Allow three to four minutes.) Other questions can be used if it is a group in which participants know one another very well:

- What is your name and where do you live?
- Tell me something about the faith community to which you belong.
- How are you feeling about this meeting?

Participants will briefly introduce their conversation partners to the group.

Invite people to share in the whole group.

- What is one hope that you have for this meeting?
- What is something that you bring to this meeting?

ROLE OF COMMUNITY GROUPS

Explain that the role of the small groups is to

- help build a sense for community
- facilitate discussion on business by involving people more closely in the process; including through the shaping of the final form of some proposals through the facilitation group process
- make it possible for the opinions of individual members to be expressed and to be heard and explored by others

In summary, the group is about community, participation, cooperation, and communication. This small group is an important part of our discernment; in listening to one another, we are also listening for the Holy Spirit.

Ask: "What values and behaviors will help us to work together well?"

Brainstorm and write a list so that everyone can see it. Ensure that each person has the chance to contribute ideas. Examples can be drawn from other places and offered to the group. For example: Rev. Eric Law offers these guidelines for respectful communication based on his work across many cultural groups over a few decades.

RESPECTFUL COMMUNICATION GUIDELINES

R = Take RESPONSIBILITY for what you say and feel without blaming others.

E = Use EMPATHETIC listening.

S = Be SENSITIVE to differences in communication styles.

P = PONDER what you hear and feel before you speak.

E = EXAMINE your own assumptions and perceptions.

C = Keep CONFIDENTIALITY.

T = TRUST ambiguity because we are not here to debate who is right or wrong.

Compare them with your list. Do they suggest anything that you would want to add to your list?

If the group already has a covenant on behavior, this should be reintroduced and reaffirmed.

Ask: "What is one positive attitude or behavior that you hope to contribute to his process?" Invite people to share.

It will be helpful to mention the importance of confidentiality. What is said in the group stays in the group.

BUSINESS

Introduce the business that will be processed through the small groups. Mention the group response form and that the views of the participants will be recorded on it.

Before discussing the particulars of the proposal/petition that is before the group, use some high-level questions to help people share the feelings, values, and experiences that are shaping their attitudes to the business that is before them.

These opening questions are very important in helping people hear what is important to one another and begin to think about how the concerns of the other group members might be met. If you are using an external facilitator, this person should be able to draft appropriate questions, as they will vary depending on the issue to be considered.

However, examples of opening discussion questions include: As you come to this business how are you feeling? When we get to talk about the proposal, what do you think are the most important things for us to take into account? What do you hope for our organization as it addresses this business? Do not record the answers to these questions.

They are not reported on but serve to support the next stage of the process.

Work through the response document that outlines the parts of the proposal/petition and provides space for answers. This is where the level of support for the various parts of the proposal can be explored. It is also the place where the matters raised in the earlier conversation can be explored further as the group members are asked if there is anything else that could be said or needs to happen or should be acted upon apart from what has come in the original set of words.

Complete the small-group response form and read it back to confirm that it accurately records the discussion in the group.

PRAYER AND OTHER CLOSING ACTIONS

There may be pastoral issues that have arisen that shape the prayers, or they may be focused on the work of the facilitation group and ongoing openness to the leading of the Holy Spirit.

Give the closing blessing. (This blessing and other liturgical resources may be provided to leaders, or leaders can use their own.)

SMALL-GROUP RESPONSE SHEET

GROUP # ____   LEADER: _____
MOBILE #: _____
TOPIC: _____
SMALL GROUP PROPOSAL #_____

Proposal # being discussed. This is the substantive matter before the small group. It is possible that the proposal is before the meeting without any notices of revision. If this is the case, then the following type of report sheet would be used. This pattern is followed until all the clauses are addressed and the views are documented.

	Yes	No	Abstain
Support for clause 1 of the proposal	____	____	_____

Did the group suggest other words or comments?
If so, write them here.

Support for additional words			
Support for clause 2 of the proposal	____	____	_____

Did the group suggest other words or comments?
If so, write them here.
If there are notices of revision, then they can be set alongside the substantive proposal and the opinion of the members be reported. Examples of the questions to answer when considering notices of revision include:
Support for deleting ABC
from line four of clause 3 (Proposal #)   ____   ____   _____

Did the group suggest other words or comments?
If so, write them here.

Support for adding XYZ
at the end of clause 4 (Proposal #)   ____   ____   _____
Did the group suggest other words or comments?
If so, write them here.

Support for additional words

FACILITATION GROUP REPORT TEMPLATE

In the report there is the opportunity to pivot from the first words that came in a proposal/petition and the material that went into the small groups, toward a set of words that gives the group an opportunity to hear the voice of the whole group for the first time. The report should include the following elements:

- Set the scene.

- Mention how many times the facilitation group met and for how long.

- Indicate how many small groups there were and how many response forms were received.

- Provide information about what came from the small groups.

- Move through each section of the proposal, indicating how many groups responded to this section; how many were in favor, against, and abstained. Use raw numbers or percentages, whichever will be most helpful to the audience.

- As each section is addressed, provide information about some of the additional comments that were made. Not every group will have made a comment, and those who did probably did not say exactly the same thing. However, it should be possible to mention categories of comments or themes. For example, it may be possible to say, "While there was significant opposition to this part of the proposal, many of the opposing groups indicated that changing these words or adding an additional idea would help them support the direction of the proposal."

- Provide a summary to draw the feedback together and identify trends in the responses.

- Based on the detailed work, summarize what has been heard. For example: "The proposal has significant support in most of its parts, but more work needs to be done on section B." A related comment might be: "Some groups suggested that by doing X, Y, and Z then this concern could be overcome." Another possible summary comment is: "The proposal is not supported, but there is a desire to see more work done in this area and not abandon the idea altogether." The summary has to be based on the group's best assessment of the detailed feedback that it has received.

- Offer recommendations for what the meeting should consider doing now. For example, members could consider a revised proposal that includes the parts of the original proposal that have strong support, with or without changes that further increase support, and deletes those parts that have low support or amends them in some way, or they may want a total redraft of the proposal.